GLORIOUS

Finding God's goodness in your womanhood

HOLLY SATTERTHWAITE

Authentic

First published 2025 by Authentic Media Limited,
PO Box 6326, Bletchley, Milton Keynes, MK1 9GG.
authenticmedia.co.uk

EU GPSR Authorised Representative
LOGOS EUROPE, 9 rue Nicolas Poussin, 17000, LA ROCHELLE, France
E-mail: contact@logoseurope.eu

British Library Cataloguing in Publication Data
A catalogue record for this book is available from the British Library.
ISBN: 978-1-78893-439-8
978-1-78893-440-4 (e-book)

Cover design by Vivian Hansen

In this soul-stirring journey through the female experience, *Glorious* offers a fresh and inspiring exploration of how God's unstoppable goodness shines through every stage and experience of womanhood. Steering away from moralistic life lessons, Holly has brought the narratives of the biblical women alive and gives every woman a powerful vision for how God's greatness shines through their current chapter in life. Essential and inspiring reading for any woman.

Debby Wright, national director of
Vineyard Churches UK & Ireland

Glorious is a wonderful devotional book, taking the reader on a journey with eleven women from the Bible. Although familiar stories, Holly has managed to bring them to life and cause their stories to impact our stories, showing that whatever season of life we are in, God can use us to reflect his glory.

Killy John, partner in ministry with J. John

This intriguing book thoughtfully and courageously handles these biblical narratives with both compassion and provocation, and a genuine desire to help contemporary women. I hope it will be widely read and bring treasures to ponder into women's lives.

Wendy Virgo, author and partner in ministry with
Terry Virgo (NewFrontiers)

Holly brings insight and depth to women in the Bible as these women reveal God's glory. God's love, compassion, purity, gentleness, power and much more are highlighted through thoughtful, faithful exposition of Scripture. Holly draws out the amazing glory of God in the lives of a diverse group of Old and New Testament women – Jewish, Gentile, old, young, those with social standing as well as the outcast. As you read, you will be brought closer to the Lord, marvel at his glory, and be inspired to live for him. In addition, the questions at the end of each chapter will further challenge you to reveal more of God's glory in your own story and to impact your family, relationships, church, workplace and community with who God is and the good news of salvation in Christ.

Elinor Magowan, FIEC director for women's ministry

Glorious is an insightful body of work which helps us to explore an alternative narrative that is really rather crucial.

Tola Doll Fisher, creative director and editor of
Premier Woman Alive, *author of* Still Standing:
100 Lessons from an Unsuccessful Life

Insightful. Wise. Refreshing. Well-written. Sometimes stretching. Always pastoral. I loved this book!

Lizzie Ling, associate minister for women at St Ebbes Church,
Oxford, UK and author of Talking Points: Abortion

Holly so uniquely brings unity to the journey of being a female follower of God. Her style disarms professional, economic and cultural differences and spotlights the shared experience we have in failure, joy, hope, redemption power and love as we journey with God.

Lisa Cuss, LPCC clinical mental health counsellor and
CapableLife.me coach

For Anna and Isaac,
Who bring us abundant joy.
May you always know how greatly loved you are.

Contents

Acknowledgements

This book would not exist without the faithful encouragement and advice of my wonderful husband, Howard Satterthwaite. You not only spoke the hope I needed to keep going and made space in our family life for me to write this, but you are also the reason I could have ever attempted it. I am always grateful for the ways in which we live and serve as a team, and how much I have learned from you. It's through your teaching, encouragement and the sharing of your own process of study that I have learned to study and teach the Bible myself. You lift me up and push me forward. You also bring all the fun and silliness any home could ever want.

Second, I want to thank my wonderful family. My parents, Robert and Tracy, have been an incredible support both practically and emotionally. I hit the parent jackpot with you both, and I'm so grateful for all you do. Spending time with you is like bathing in love. God has also blessed me with a wonderfully supportive sister-in-law and parents-in-law who I know have prayed for me throughout this journey.

Life wouldn't be much fun without friends to share it with, and I am honoured to have always been surrounded by girls and then women who have made seeing God's revelation through womanhood easy. I am truly grateful to also have a handful of 'Jonathans' who have in many ways inspired some of this book – you know who you are. You have helped me see God's goodness in the dark as well as the light and carried me when my own feet failed me. Your enduring kindness is a gift I will always treasure. Thank you that despite distance, circumstances (and my mood or communication frequency) for some reason you still choose me as a friend. Your friendship is so precious, and without it I couldn't have finished this project.

Thank you to Authentic Media for taking a punt on this book project and being so kind and encouraging in the process; for being excited about it, when I was letting my apprehension start to take centre stage. I am so grateful for your work in bringing this book through to completion.

Lastly, and most importantly, thank you to my Heavenly Father who has loved me so perfectly and saved me so beautifully. Thank you for your grace and mercy, and that you are so glorious and good that it needed another book in the world to explain it.

Introduction

The week I started writing this book, I walked my youngest child to the school gates for the first time. Feeling the warmth of his soft little hand in mine, I let go and left him there, thereby graduating from the ranks of exhausted preschool mum to some new, as yet uncertain league of motherhood. Having spent countless hours sitting in the kids' playpark on a bench that became so familiar it's like an extension of my living-room, it now feels oddly inappropriate to visit it on my own. So, instead, I sat in my actual living-room and, having spent over seven years dreaming of this moment, it felt gut-wrenchingly quiet.

Life is full of seasons. In some ways, it's one long transition or learning journey as we who know Christ move toward eternity. Hopefully we are becoming more Christlike and bringing more of his sweet fragrance to our different settings. Regardless of whether we marry or have kids, live in plenty or scrape together a living, we all grow, love and struggle. We win, and we lose. We learn, and sometimes we ignorantly refuse to. We are all living out our stories with experiences and personalities as diverse as creation itself, and yet there is a common and distinct bond in womanhood to which I can't adequately put words. It's an understanding that spans generations and history and, weaved through them all, through the ever-changing experience of women, is the expression of God's unchanging glory.

For some, 'God's glory' may conjure up images of dominion and subjugation, inaccessible beauty or dramatic acts that perforate an otherwise boring and insignificant life. That is not what God is like. In Exodus 33:18 Moses pleads with God to 'Please show me your glory'. God's response is not a Zeus-like roar of thunder but, instead, 'I will make all my goodness pass before you' (Exod. 33:19). God defines his glory not in terms of oppressive power but in terms of his goodness.[1] In Exodus 34:6–7 he describes himself as 'merciful and gracious, slow to anger, and abounding in steadfast love and faithfulness, keeping steadfast love for thousands, forgiving iniquity and transgression and sin, but who will by no means clear the guilty, visiting the iniquity of the fathers on the children and the children's children, to the third and the fourth generation'.

What we see expressed through every person's story is an invitation into awe and relationship with the unchanging goodness of a personal God who mercifully loves us. This book explores the different stories, seasons and themes that we experience as women, and how God's glory shines through each of them.

The biblical women we will look at were women just like you. They struggled with marital challenges, difficult friendships, fertility, grief and unfulfilled dreams. They were compassionate, generous, hospitable, jealous, proud and controlling. They came in all shapes and sizes, just like modern women today. Some of their narratives don't make for easy reading. Life isn't easy and the Bible is shockingly honest about that and the reality of who these women were – richly complex, all tainted by sin, with mixed motives and cultural pressures. These are real people, just like you and me.

As we journey through the scriptural narratives of these biblical women, I think they invite us to consider three main things: they prompt us to make the choice; they encourage and strengthen us; and they teach us about God's character.

Biblical women prompt us to make *the* choice

A few years ago, just after we moved to Central London, we walked up the road to Parliament Square to show our daughter, Anna, the newly unveiled statue of Millicent Fawcett. Millicent, if you don't know her, was a key leader of the Suffragist movement who tirelessly campaigned for women to get the vote in the UK. Much of the history we explained went over our 4-year-old daughter's head, but it was important to us that she grew up knowing that her voice matters, that she has value and a valuable contribution to make to our country. This country sees her, and she has a responsibility to choose wisely how she reacts to that. The parliamentary voting acts of 1918 and 1928 changed the face of UK politics as women slowly but surely gained the vote, and altered our country as we gradually saw greater and better legislation around education, welfare, maternal health and equality of pay, just to mention a few areas. It would be simplistic and harsh to argue that men before 1928 didn't care about such things. I'm sure some did deeply, but the catalyst for change seems to have been the choice of women to use the new power they had to engage with the work and influence of the government.

Why am I sharing this story? Our government has given our daughter, and all citizens, the power to be a part of the working out of democracy in our country. It's our choice what part we play in that story. God has also given us a choice, in whether or how we partner with him. Unlike democracy, his kingdom cannot be stopped. Psalm 46:10 declares: 'Be still, and know that I am God. I *will* be exalted among the nations, I *will* be exalted in the earth!' He is sovereign, and his glory, gospel and purposes continue regardless of our choice, as we will discover through some of the biblical narratives in this book. His glory *will* be expressed in our story, but he is inviting us to play our part in how. It can shine through his provision in light of our dependence on him, or his humbling of us in the face of our pride and doomed attempts at self-sufficiency. How will God's glory show in your story?

They encourage and strengthen us

As we study the narratives of these biblical women, we will find connection with our heartaches, temptations and joys. There is a fellowship between believers that extends beyond time – a friend once told me that some of her best friends are dead Christian authors. Reading Scripture is a rich reminder of God's faithfulness and consistency to generation after generation across all times, cultures and nations. It shows us that we are not alone and that our struggles and wrestling is nothing new. We never journey with God in isolation; through church past and present we have a shared experience of failure, forgiveness and joy. One day we will not know these deceased authors and believers as the names of dead people on a page but as resurrected friends with whom we will spend eternity, sharing our stories of God's mercy and grace.

The honest portrayals of these biblical women can also help us to live more authentic expressions of our own lives. Too often, we are caught in a comparison or insecurity trap, exchanging specially crafted personas with each other rather than the real, raw, inner us. How often do you choose a filter for your social media posts? Or angle the camera to exclude the mess in the corner? I have shared beautiful smiling photos of my family, miraculously captured in the middle of a grumpy tantrum-filled day – yet that aspect stays out of the description. When I was a self-employed coach, I talked about the work I had rather than the days that went by anxiously quiet without client meetings. We think it will protect us, but it just discourages ourselves, intimidates others, and feeds the lie that we need to hide our true selves. And the more we hide, the more power we give the devil to nurture our fears and sin under the secret cover of darkness.

The Bible doesn't give the scriptural women the luxury of keeping any constructed filter. It lifts the lid and shows them – warts, smiles and all. In doing so, we can learn from them, be encouraged to persevere, and not lose heart when we falter. You are not alone in your faith journey or struggle with sin and disappointment. What a difference it might make if we, too, could drop our filters and be living narratives, encouraging others with how God's glory has worked out in our joy and darkness. After all, the purpose of life is not for others to bask in our glory but in his.[2]

They teach us about God's character

With what lens(es) do you approach the Bible? I so clearly remember the morning of my interview for Cambridge University (spoiler alert: I didn't get a place). I was only the second person in my family, after my cousin, to go to university, and I was so nervous. I felt the weight of my family's sacrifices to get me to this point and the terror of stepping into completely unknown territory. So what does any new and immature believer do in such a situation? I grabbed my Bible and flung it open onto a random page while asking God to speak to me, to tell me what I should do and what was going to happen. The verse that my blindfolded, finger-flinging approach took me to was: 'He was oppressed, and he was afflicted, yet he opened not his mouth; like a lamb that is led to the slaughter, and like a sheep that before its shearers is silent, so he opened not his mouth' (Isa. 53:7). This verse could have been a source of great comfort and strengthening but I was still under the deluded impression that the Bible was primarily about me. I took this as a prediction of doom. No one will ever know if my interview would have gone differently had I better understood this verse, but it certainly felt prophetic by the time it was over! (And this is no criticism of the university but rather my inadequate preparation.)

What if we aren't the centre of the biblical story? When we read our Bibles, we often look for quick takeaways to find out what we should do or who we should be rather than who God is. I think this can sometimes be a challenge with the passages about or involving women. What if the narratives of the biblical women weren't primarily written to tell us what a woman is, what she should do or not do? What if their purpose was not to motivate either striving or limiting but, like the rest of Scripture, to reveal God's glory to us? The Bible is rich, fragrant and layered. Yes, it has much to say about how we should live, but if we jump to 'me' too quickly, we miss out on something beautiful – God's self-revelation to us.

The Bible is all about the Father, Son and Holy Spirit, and it's in our growing understanding of who he is that we more fully discover who we are. This is what I was missing that terror-driven morning of my interview; my lens was so self-involved I missed that Isaiah 53:7 is 100 per cent about Jesus, a predicted sacrifice and suffering I will never fully comprehend, let alone endure myself. How I could have ever read that passage and not been struck with awe or rejoiced at the love of my Saviour now baffles me!

As we study the scriptural narratives of these biblical women, they are going to reveal a lot to us about the women themselves, their culture and other biblical characters. Still, the most wonderful revelation they will give us is of God himself. Behind the devotion of Anna, who spent nearly all her days in prayer and fasting at the temple before she met baby Jesus, we see an even more devoted God; the God who would send his son as a vulnerable baby to a sin-filled world to grow, teach and ultimately die to save us. Behind the courage and faithfulness of Esther to rescue her people, we discover a perfectly faithful God whose sovereign rescue plan can never be derailed.

How to read this book

We need to go on this journey together to grasp the truths, joys and encouragements of these biblical narratives. You need to engage with the texts for yourself and spend time reflecting on your own life. This gives space for the Holy Spirit to speak to you and for your heart and mind to learn and understand more deeply, rather than rushing on to the next chapter. For this reason, each chapter starts with a short Bible study and ends with a few questions for reflection.

The biblical women's stories have depths and many perspectives, so each chapter addresses one aspect or lens through which to study each woman's story. It's not the only lens;

choosing one should help you hear God's voice more clearly. In addition, the chapters mimic some of the thematic rhythms or seasons of a woman's life – growing up, periods (yep!), making decisions, unexpected endings and many more. The chapters themselves are arranged chronologically according to when we encounter the biblical women in Scripture, so that we can see how truth and our awareness of God's goodness builds through the Bible and be reminded that we are not the centre that these books revolve around. I also don't want to impose a thematic order onto your experience of womanhood. We are all different and our journeys do not often take logical routes. As I see my grey hairs stubbornly continuing to emerge, I am aware that at times I have just as much growing up to do as when my mum gave me my first face cream and bra.

You can work through these chapters on your own, perhaps as part of your devotional time with God or in small groups, reading the main chapter content in between meetups. You could savour the book reading a chapter a month, allowing the messages into the rhythm of your own story over the course of a year. It's up to you, but I would encourage you to engage with the Bible study and application questions. I know the temptation to skip over them. We're busy women trying to squeeze some devotional time into our lives but better to do less and be more. By this I mean you could finish this book in a couple of weeks and remain unchanged, or you could take your time and let your growing understanding of the Scripture and God's character totally transform you. God doesn't flip a switch when we believe in him; transformation and the realignment of our identity and self-value take time. Let's trust God with our time and learn to be vulnerable as we read his word.

1 HAGAR

Afraid of the Dark

Bible study

Read

Genesis 16; 21:1-21

Context

Following the great flood and the tower of Babel, God has chosen Abraham and Sarah to be the beginning of his chosen people who will build a huge nation that will be a blessing to all the families of the earth. In Genesis 15, God makes a covenantal promise with Abraham on this basis. Abraham and Sarah have no children at this point in the narrative.

Study and write

- How does God's treatment of Hagar contrast with Abraham and Sarah's?

- In what ways have Sarah and Abraham doubted God and sinned against him?

Pray and reflect

- How easy do you find it to wait for God to do what he has promised? Reflect on the ways in which you are waiting on God to move in your life and invite him to help you to wait well.

- Are there any moments when you feel overwhelmed or in despair? Tell God about these situations and ask him to show you that he is with you.

Thoughts on Hagar

Fear may seem like an unusual chapter topic to begin a book with, but I think there is a reason that the chronological order of the stories we're looking at took us to this narrative first. I have never met a woman that hasn't felt held back by fear at some point. Be it in reality or imagined in anxious minds, about harm or humiliation, fear is endemic in our womanhood and it distracts us from joy and purpose. To truly see God's glory, we need to learn to face and look beyond our fear to accept the invitation into awe and courage. So, let's stand hand in hand with Jesus and face the darkness square on . . .

I was scared of the dark for an embarrassingly long time as a child. Huddled with my night-light and teddies, I wasted countless hours fearing the unreal – monsters hidden in my wardrobe or strangers skulking in the shadows underneath my bed. I thought that as I grew up I would learn to embody the phrase all parents use to their children on tired late nights: 'There is nothing to be afraid of.' The reality has been, though, that my unreal skulking strangers were replaced with real-life strangers who followed me home after late nights at the office or shouted crude comments at me in the street. I'm not alone; UK Government studies show that 82 per cent of women are afraid to be in a park or open public space after dark and 50 per cent on a quiet street near their home.[1] My wardrobe turned out to be safe after all, but other trusted places and relationships repeatedly let me down with jealous, unkind or offensive comments.

I am under no illusion that my life has been privileged and loved in many ways to date; however, even in that bubble of care I am very aware of the darkness that lurks around. There are people who keep poking, maybe hoping to burst it, and events that conspire to wound. Sometimes it feels that even creation itself is working against us – perhaps you know the loss caused by a flood. I think of my daughter nearly drowning in a swimming pool at the age of 3 and my son choking on some food at 8 months – can it be that even food and water can't be trusted?

There are those who know the destruction of this darkness far better than I do. Sana is an Iraqi Christian. I heard of her story through the work of Open Doors, who work to support and learn from the witness of the persecuted church around the world. When so-called Islamic State took the Iraqi city of Qaraqosh in 2014, she was forcibly removed from her home and her family separated. Ten years later she still doesn't know what happened to her husband and sons. Her story is one of pain, grief and anger. Sana, supported by Open Doors partners, began to open up to trusted believers and to God about her distress. She began to find hope and an incredible strength in knowing God's presence with her. Where is Sana now? She's still displaced. She still knows nothing of her husband and sons. She is still not safe in her home city.

Life is as hard as it is beautiful. Fear is not always rooted in a weak, anxious heart but it can be an objective and rational response to the fallen reality we all build our lives within. God does not, after all, promise us safety in this life. In fact, he's pretty clear that we will encounter plenty of difficulties. Sin is defeated but it still lurks around us, and in us, until Jesus returns.

This is a truth that Hagar knew very well. Hers is a hard narrative to swallow because it cuts against how we assume God's goodness will work in our #bestlifenow culture. She is mistreated and her suffering doesn't abate after her encounter with God: he is with her, *and* life is still hard. That's also why her story resonates so deeply, because life will always have something hard or fear-inducing for us to grapple with or hiding just around the corner. God's aim was never for us to completely escape the hard in this life, but to find him in it.

Hagar – an Egyptian servant belonging to Sarai – had been brought into a family with a big promise over them. God had repeatedly told Abram that he and Sarai would birth a great nation that would be a blessing to all the earth. This was the beginning of Israel, God's people, whom he had chosen to dwell with and work through. However, years later when Sarai was advanced in age, they still hadn't conceived. At this point Hagar's life changed when Sarai gave her to Abram to have a baby on her behalf. To be honest, culturally for the region, this would have been a perfectly proper and respectable course of action for people in the ancient Near East who weren't living within our social norms, which are saturated with the inheritance of Christian values. But God was creating something new with Sarai and Abram, and this went against the model of marriage and human flourishing he had established since creation when Eve and Adam were given to each other. It went against the truth, which Abram and Sarai should have known (and probably did), that we are all made in God's image and so each person is to be cherished.

Abram's sin against Hagar, in agreeing and going along with Sarai's plan in Genesis 16:1–2, was one of violence, but it wasn't purely one of lust. We're not told that Abram desired

Hagar over Sarai, but rather it seems that the couple had fundamentally lost their faith in God's ability or willingness to act on his promise to provide them with a son. Reminiscent of Adam and Eve and the fall in Genesis 3, Abram and Sarai doubted God and what he had said. In Genesis 16:2 Sarai declares: 'Behold now, the LORD has prevented me from bearing children', which is the exact opposite of what God had said he would do for Abram. They had lost confidence in God being as good or powerful as he had claimed to be.

Sarai, caught up in the shame and disappointment that we all struggle with in the lengthy waiting place between God's promise and its fulfilment, anxiously strove so hard to give Abram what he was meant to have that 'she becomes forgetful of her own right'.[2] God's promise to Abram was never for him alone. As his agency for delivering this nation of multitudes was through children and marriage, it was always a promise for Sarai too. This is seen when God reaffirms his promise and honours Sarai with a new name, Sarah, in Genesis 17:15–16 after Ishmael's birth. God declares, 'she shall become nations; kings of peoples shall come from her' (Gen. 17:16) as he highlights the centrality of her role with Abram. Both were chosen to bring forth God's chosen nation. Ishmael could never have fulfilled God's prophecy because his conception had sidestepped the woman God had chosen for this task, which was far larger than conceiving a baby but would require nurturing a whole people to know God and follow his voice.

I think this is key to why Sarah[3] mistreated Hagar so much. If it had solely come from a place of jealousy about having a child, you might expect it to have abated once Isaac was born. Instead, it seems only to intensify. Sarah is jealous of Ishmael and the joy he brings Abraham, but I wonder if she is also crippled with anxiety because she fears that, by her actions, she has removed herself and Isaac from the great blessing and adventure that God had promised them. Interestingly, the Hebrew word for 'dealt harshly with her' in Genesis 16:6, '*anah*, signifies a humbling within the context of affliction. It seems that rather than repent and face reality, Sarah redirects the anger she feels against herself and releases it instead on the individuals that reflect back to her the undeniable existence of her own sin. Is this why, in Genesis 21, she invokes this divine promise to justify her desire to cast out Ishmael and Hagar? It's clear from history that children born to slave-wives could inherit with children of the primary wife, and in this case Sarah is keen to grant Hagar and Ishmael their freedom so that they would forfeit this claim. She wanted to make sure that the great story of provision and faith told in the generations to come would be of Sarah and Abraham, not Hagar and Abraham.

Sarah did not mean this for good, but God used it to bring about his purposes and blessing for Isaac and Ishmael. Incredibly, Sarah, even despite this awful sin and disbelief, could not remove herself from the gift of blessing that God had promised to her. Despite her inability to right the wrong she'd done, she didn't need to be afraid of her own darkness. God's steadfast commitment to Sarah may jar with our sense of justice, but it is a picture of the grace that all believers now dwell under – a grace that we all, like Sarah, desperately need.

That doesn't mean that God forgot Hagar. Sin, however beautifully forgiven, still has consequences and ripples for those around us. God knows this and, rather than cast her out as Sarah had done, he drew close to her. Genesis 16 and 21 illustrate the intimate goodness of God when life is heavy and overwhelming. In these chapters we find that, even when life remains hard, through God we are known, blessed and provided for.

Known

When the darkness closes in, whether that be our own sin, sickness or other's actions, one of the most common tricks of the devil is to convince us that we are alone. If we are over-looked, unnecessary, abandoned or invisible in any way then God cannot be love, and the light of his goodness is easily quashed. Yet, that is a lie.

In Genesis 16:7–8, Hagar has run away from the mistreat-ment she has received from Sarah, and she is in the wilder-ness. She has removed herself from community and is fleeing through a desolate land, and yet even during this physical iso-lation, she is not alone. In fact, it's here that God seems clos-est to her. The passage says that the angel of the Lord 'found her', and (after she and Ishmael are banished) Genesis 21:17 says that God heard Ishmael's cries and the angel called out to Hagar in the wilderness. As she pulls away in reaction to hurt, God's reaction is to pull her close to himself. It's as if he makes himself more visible at the moments when she feels most in-visible. 'Flee sin, but don't flee me' seems to be his motto. Just as Sarah's own sin couldn't exclude herself from God's good-ness, it also can't exclude Hagar. Even when everyone seems to have rejected us, God still desires to be with us.

God is also the only one who calls Hagar by her name in Scripture. While she's referred to generically as 'servant' or 'slave woman' and never spoken to by Sarah or Abraham but rather is spoken about, God speaks directly to her through his angel and addresses her by name (Gen. 16:8; 21:17). To others Hagar was defined by her role or position (with her name literally meaning 'flight, emigration or forsaken'), but to God she was known as her unique self. While, at this time and place, Hagar would have been treated as property to be owned and used as needed, God knows her as the child he created and values her emotions and wellbeing.[4] In contrast to the displaced and unknown theme of her name's meaning, God roots her in his care, with deep understanding of who she is and her future.

Hagar is not only not alone, but she is more deeply known by God than she knows herself. In Genesis 16, God tells her she's pregnant with a son and gives some insight into what his life will be like in the future. It's in response to this that she exclaims, 'You are a God of seeing' (Gen. 16:13). The seeing and hearing in these chapters aren't just about eyeballs and ear-holes, they are an expression of the deepest form of understanding and compassion. This is why Hagar could go back to Sarah and Abraham in Genesis 16 – a command that feels impossibly hard to us. She had the strength to trust God and return because he knew her. He knew her future and all that she was running from; he knew it all and he was good. If he knew that much, then she could trust him that he also knew what he was doing by sending her back. It wasn't a mistake or a questionable choice. It wasn't a misdiagnosis of the problem. The only reaction to this omniscience was not to question, but to be overcome with awe – a fearsome awe.

The way to fight against our fear of the dark is to embrace a fear of the light: the fear of God. This fear doesn't control us but is rather birthed and mingled in love – like a child for their parent. While the dark diminishes and limits us, a fear of

God gives courage, hope and strength. It is a good, clean fear that rallies us like warriors about to roar into battle that our lives, however difficult or short-lived, will not be wasted or without purpose. It's a fear that opens our eyes to the beauty and connectedness of life and eternity. It's like when we watch NASA images of faraway galaxies and we catch a glimpse of just how breathtaking and vast the universe is, and yet it somehow makes our tiny part of it feel even more precious and meaningful rather than less. As we stand in awe and trepidation of all we don't know, we also feel a swell of joy and love for what and whom we do, and the One who gave them to us. It's a reverent fear that comes from recognizing something, or someone, so good, so perfect and magnificent that we realize how unworthy we are to be in their presence.

Such a fear, a fear of God, overwhelmed Hagar's fear of the darkness that might await her back with Sarah and Abraham. She knew that a direct request from the awesome God who loved her and knew all could only be the right thing to do, even when she must have hoped for another route.

It's also important to note that by sending Hagar back, God was not endorsing the treatment she received from Sarah or Abraham. God saw Sarah's anxiety and shame, but he also saw her jealous cruelty. He saw Abraham's guilt in doing nothing to abate that cruelty, even aiding and abetting it as he failed to see the beloved humanity also within Hagar. The Bible makes no attempt to rose-tint the couple's actions even though they are his chosen people. They are there for us all to read for millennia. At the time, Hagar must have felt powerless and isolated, yet through God's inclusion of it within Scripture her suffering has been and will be known and empathized with for generations.

Blessed

Talking about blessing seems out of step with the ordeal Hagar went through. It can feel like language reserved for those being promoted, having babies or building extensions. My mind bursts with humble-brag hashtags online from beautiful young believers who have yet to realize how brutal life can and will be. And yet, recently when I found myself standing among the ashes of a life seemingly burnt to the ground, it was the practice of blessing – finding and inviting God's goodness and grace into whatever lies before me – that saved me from crumbling along with all the pillars of security I had previously taken for granted. Could it be that even as we walk through the fire, though it may painfully burn, God and his desire to bless his children will always be there with us?

Throughout these passages, in contrast to the conduct of people, God's blessing of goodness and grace floods the pages. These are not unhelpful silver linings or flat words of encouragement, instead the One who knows the true depths of our grief and sorrow knows how to give the exact kindness and blessing that we need.

We have already touched on the radical grace shown to Sarah by God persisting in his promise to build a great nation through her, despite her abuse of Hagar and lack of faith in God's ability or willingness to follow through on what he had said.

I am also struck by God's solution to the conflict between the two women and their inability to live together (Hagar was not an entirely innocent party – she does seem to have lorded her pregnancy over Sarah and been difficult with her). It reminds me of my first home and the challenges we had with a disruptive neighbour who would blast expletive R 'n' B music until 3 a.m. As I watched our windows shake and the hours tick on, my angst would grow as I prayed that the police would intervene, or other neighbours might challenge her. In the end, God acted not with the judgement or punishment that was in my heart but with grace. He solved the impasse with goodness: the house prices in our area experienced an unexpected, extraordinary surge and our impoverished neighbour sold her flat and bought a bigger, nicer place somewhere else. We found sleep and quiet, and she found a family home for her kids.

In the same way, God solves the conflict between Sarah and Hagar as they grapple for supremacy and ownership of this great, good promise for Abraham's family with more great, good promises. While Sarah looked on life with a mindset of scarcity and believed that she needed to hoard the blessing for Isaac, God's goodness wasn't limited or bound to just one promise or one route to blessing. His covenant promise with Abraham was for Isaac, but that didn't mean that one child must be left unblessed. In the words of John Calvin, 'God intended that a monument of the paternal kindness, with which he embraced the whole house of Abram, should endure to prosperity.'5 Accordingly, God extends a new promise of a nation of multitudes to Hagar in Genesis 16, which Ishmael will inherit. This provided for Ishmael the favour and freedom that Hagar had longed for.

When Hagar and Ishmael were sent away in Genesis 21, they relinquished their right to inheritance within Abraham's family and Ishmael lost the biological father who clearly cared for him. However, God makes it clear that being excluded from *this* family didn't mean that they were excluded from *his* family. He would be with Ishmael and there was always an open invitation for Ishmael from his Eternal Father who loved him.

This brings us to the harder blessing for Hagar to receive: the blessing of God's people. As I have wrestled with God's decision to send her back to Sarah and Abraham in Genesis 16, it is this blessing, seen in the light of God's unwavering goodness, that most helps me find peace with this command. Throughout Scripture, God sets a principle that it is always best for us to stay within God's family (today, the church). These days, in the UK, we have a plethora of local churches with different styles and cultures to choose from, to find our fit and a healthy place within the kingdom of God. Back in Genesis 16, that kingdom on earth was still at its infant stages and Abraham's family was the extent of God's chosen people.

God's church is a core mechanism by which God wants us to learn about and draw close to himself; to be shaped and sharpened, loved and supported. How did Hagar, an Egyptian servant, recognize the voice of God and his messenger so quickly? How did she know about him at all? Surely it has come from being part of Abraham's household and hearing about his covenant promises and how God has already spoken to him. Even in the dysfunction of this family, she has experienced some discipleship that has drawn her to God, and God's desire is for all people to come to know him and be blessed through this family. So, when he finds her on the way to Shur, in the direction of her homeland Egypt, he calls her back not solely to Sarah, but back to his kingdom and where he is choosing to dwell. The message is, 'Don't flee from me and return to your old ways. Don't give up on me because of my people's sin.'

That does not undermine the seriousness of the sin, but rather elevates the radicalness of God's grace. In fact, the sin against Hagar is so much more than originally meets the eye because it was perpetrated by God's chosen people. When God promised that Abraham and Sarah would be the beginning of a generation that would bring God's blessings to the whole world, they got so fixated on questions of fertility that they missed the fact that the promise had already started. It didn't start with Isaac, it started with them the moment that the prophecy was given. They were meant to be bringing blessing to 'all the families of the earth' (Gen. 12:3).

In this blessing there is a long-term prophecy that will pave a lineage all the way to Christ, but there is also an immediate responsibility on them too. As we see later when the law is given, this embryonic group of God's people were meant to look after the foreigner and widow and provide for the most vulnerable in their midst – to mimic God's character in how they interacted with those around them. Instead, Sarah and Abraham fell at the first hurdle. Hagar, a vulnerable foreigner in their household, is not blessed by them but mistreated and exiled into the wilderness rather than provided for.

'All the families of the earth' is not some unnamed collective living at arm's length; it is made up of multitudes of unique, divinely created and loved individuals. Families like Hagar and Ishmael, whom God intimately knew and saw. The reason why Hagar's mistreatment was so unbearable is because it came from the very people God had chosen to bring her and her people blessing, the people who were meant to be family to her. This is why church hurt, which most of us will experience at some point, is so much deeper and rawer than any hurt that the 'world' or individual unbelievers can do to us.

And yet, even in light of this, the angel of God says, 'Return to your mistress and submit to her' (Gen. 16:9). It's an act of great grace that God gives Abraham and Sarah another chance to be his people to Hagar and get it right. I think that by asking this of Hagar, God asked her to share in the same radical forgiveness that he had shown to them. Rather than being abusively humbled, she is asked to submit – a choice that comes from choosing to love the other. As a foreshadow of Matthew 5:43–4, Hagar is to do good to those who hate her and bless those who curse her. Such a reaction God describes as 'a glorious thing' (1 Pet. 2:19).

If anyone can sympathize with Hagar's return, it's Jesus. God is not a hypocrite. He is also willing to silently suffer at the hands of his own people in order to bring his blessing to all the earth. In Luke 22:42–4, Jesus calls out to God the night before his crucifixion, '"Father, if you are willing, remove this cup from me. Nevertheless, not my will, but yours, be done." And there appeared to him an angel from heaven, strengthening him. And being in agony he prayed more earnestly; and his sweat became like great drops of blood falling down to the ground.' This haematidrosis can occur in individuals suffering from extreme levels of stress.[6] Jesus knew fear. Interestingly, scientists believe that the rupture of the blood vessels happens not during the stress but as the anxiety passes and, in this passage, it seems that Jesus sweated blood after the angel from heaven arrived to strengthen him. God may call us to seemingly impossibly hard things, but he will never leave us alone without the strength to do them.

It's important to note that when Sarah and Abraham don't change their ways, God creates a way out for Hagar and Ishmael. None of us should stay forever in abusive positions, including when the mistreatment is coming from other believers in a church environment, but God asks us not to walk out on him in the process.

In the same way, the corporate church has things in its collective history which are painfully outrageous betrayals and yet God has not given up on the church. It is still his rescue plan and hope for the world, and he asks us to show it the same grace that he shows it. For a while, this grace was the only way I could physically stand in a church. I know church hurt. But I also know that I am known by a good God who knows me better than I know myself and he tells me that this imperfect vehicle, this ramshackle collection of loving and occasionally unkind, humble and yet also arrogant, selfless and simultaneously self-serving believers, is where I am meant to be. They are what is best for me and so I have learned, through faith, to trust him . . . even when the dark creeps in.

Provisioned

Walking closely with God through the darkness doesn't earn us points that we can redeem like some coupon system. We don't get to submit our shopping lists of life to God and see each of them ticked off, but he does promise to supply all our needs.[7] He will provide, according to his wisdom and not ours, what we need in order to keeping putting one foot in front of the other and find abundance in him.

God provides not just promises for Hagar, but also material provisions. In Genesis 21, in contrast to the meagre bread and *skin of water* that Abraham sent her and Ishmael into the wilderness with, God opens her eyes to see a *well of water* that he has provided for her and her son. A well, being a symbol of abundance and life throughout the Bible, meets her immediate need at the same time as reassuring her of God's reliability to continue to sustain them. Ishmael stayed in the wilderness as he grew, and built his family and nation. The desert region of Negev was a difficult place in which to find water, but it seems that God provided a constant supply of food and water for Hagar and Ishmael even in this barren place. As they built a new life together with literally nothing, God gave them all they needed. We, like Hagar in that grief-filled moment, don't know how, but we see his first step as a proof to trust him for the rest. We often don't see the whole picture, but God loves to lead us step by step, one skin of water by one skin of water, to a place of flourishing.

God also provides relationally for Hagar. In Genesis 16:11, he tells her that she will have a son, and Ishmael certainly turns out to be *Hagar's* son. While Sarah had intended that she would obtain children for Abraham through Hagar (Gen. 16:2), in Genesis 16:15 Abraham publicly names the boy 'Ishmael'. Abraham must have allowed Hagar to choose his name, given that it had been given to her by God alone. Naming someone or something was an important, almost sacred, act in the Old Testament that often signified owner-ship or authority: in Genesis 21, Ishmael is referred to not as Sarah's but 'the son of Hagar the Egyptian . . . the son of this slave woman' (Gen. 21:9–10).

Later, in Genesis 21:21, we are told that Hagar chose a wife for Ishmael. This is a poignant inclusion as it was normally a role the father would undertake. It underscores Ishmael's sep-aration from Abraham, at the same time as reinforcing Hagar's commitment to her son. Sarah had intended Ishmael to be born for herself, but he has truly become Hagar's and hers alone as the Egyptian woman takes on the full parental role for him.[8] Through this responsibility, God has provided for Hagar a loyal and loving family unit that she could never have had in Abraham's household – a family that will bring her joy and care for her now and in her later years.

Most importantly, God provides his presence and grace to all of them. The family who rejected, and the family who were rejected. Though both will flourish and grow on opposite sides of the coin, separated, God's presence doesn't have to choose between the two. He promises to build with Ishmael too, and Genesis 21:20 tells us that 'God was with the boy'. God had a divine promise for Isaac, but Isaac's promise (unearned but gifted) didn't diminish Ishmael in God's sight. I am struck by how fairly God treats the boys, and Abraham's fatherhood in relation to each son. In Genesis 21:12–14, Abraham is told to entrust beloved Ishmael's life into God's hands and send him away vulnerable and helpless into the wilderness. Similarly, in the very next chapter in Genesis following this, God asks Abraham to take Isaac and offer him as a burnt offering on one of the mountains. God knew that at the last minute he would provide a lamb to replace Isaac, but he wanted to test Abraham and teach him to entrust God with Isaac's life in the same way as he had Ishmael's. Abraham was forced to entrust both sons into God's care. Both grew up with God's presence and equally within the security and love of his hands.

Lastly, God provided a future for Hagar and Ishmael when all Hagar saw ahead was certain death (Gen. 21:16–18). At times, we can be so crushed by the weight of grief or the instability of life that feeling anything other than despair seems impossible. The darkness can get so dark that we struggle to see the flicker of the future God has promised us. And yet, however distant, light is always coming.

Hagar's life is a metaphor for our walk as believers: hold fast to him and to his chosen community, the church, even among the buffeting and hardship of living in a world reeling and twisted by the impact of sin, because God is with us. He knows us, he will bless us and provide for us, and he has a future for us in the next life which overflows in freedom and abundance. Unlike in Hagar's life before the resurrection of Jesus, we don't need to have offspring to find that freedom. God has already provided his own son to secure it for us.

As God relentlessly pursues his creation, we are part of a battle between light and dark for the souls of the earth. In every battle there is hard exhausting work, injury and even death. But once this battle is over and we stand in our assured victory, we have a promised future of forever with God without any danger or suffering as part of the greatest nation, the kingdom of God. One day, the time of darkness will be over, 'And night will be no more. They will need no light of lamp or sun, for the Lord God will be their light, and they will reign for ever and ever' (Rev. 22:5). So, sleep tight, little girls who keep checking under the bed; walk bravely, young ladies making your way home in the dark; and love in abundance, women weathered by life, because darkness will not have the final say and your future is blazing brightly.

Questions for reflection

What is the darkness that most scares you at the moment?

How does the fear of God give you courage and hope?

In what ways do you know God's blessing right now?

In what ways have you known God's miraculous provision, and how do you need his provision now?

2

JOCHEBED

I am Mother, Hear Me Roar

Bible study

Read

Exodus 2:1-10; Hebrews 11:23

Context

The Israelites have grown hugely in number in Egypt and, worried about the consequences were they to revolt, the new Pharaoh has made them slaves and is working them ruthlessly. He has ordered the Hebrew midwives to kill every male Hebrew baby born. However, the midwives fear God and don't do as they were commanded, allowing the baby boys to live. Pharaoh has now commanded that every son born to the Hebrews should be cast into the Nile (Exod.1:1).

Study and write

- What role does each character take in this story? (Jochebed and Amran, Miriam, Pharoah's daughter, Moses and God)

- What themes of motherhood do we see reflected in this narrative?

- What gave Jochebed and Amran hope for their son?

Pray and reflect

- Think about how your approach to love has been influenced by the role of your mother in your life (both positively and negatively).

- Thank God for the good examples of motherhood you have known and invite God to bring healing to where motherhood causes you pain.

Thoughts on Jochebed

I wonder what the word 'motherhood' conjures up in your mind. Some of you may feel as though you are right in the trenches of raising sticky-fingered toddlers or emotionally complex teenagers. For some of you, the word elicits a sting of longing, the devastation of loss or an indifferent apathy to a future you can't quite picture. For others of you, just the fact that this is the second chapter in this book will sit uneasily with you. Rest assured; this chapter is for all of you.

These pages are not a lesson in child-rearing – you'll find no discipline or weaning tips here – but rather an exploration of the often-overlooked maternal love that God so frequently leans upon to explain the depth of his devotion to us. Don't get me wrong, God is *Father*, Son and Holy Spirit. Throughout the Bible it is clearly taught that God is Father.[1] But within this divine fatherhood is a love so deep that the Scriptures turn to motherhood to help us understand it. Male and female, we are created in his image, and both are needed to reflect that image. In this way, we cannot properly begin to understand the supernaturally perfect love of God the Father without the presence of motherhood in the world.

To explore this, we are going to need to start by talking about biological mothering in Scripture – birthing, boobs and bears. But I want to be clear from the outset, that mothers come in many forms (adoptive, spiritual, biological, step-mothers, etc.) and all of these are worthy, wonderful workings out of motherhood. This exploration of Scripture is not meant in any way to pedestal biological mothers above others. It is also not meant to suggest that the love of a mother is better or greater than the love of a father. My husband loves our children with a passion and sacrificial heart that inspires me. Rather, I propose that, to understand the nature of the love that God has for us, we need to see the messages he has written into our biology as women and how Scripture calls us to take notice of them.

I know that might be difficult reading for those of you who are in the middle of the anguish of not having the children you desire or having lost the children you loved. I will try to take you on this journey gently, but along it I think you will be comforted by a love from God that is deeper than you could ever have imagined.

Jochebed

When I was a teenager, I saw the film *Seven Pounds*[2] with my mum at the cinema. The premise of the film is that the main character is going to die but wants to help others with his organs and is seeking out worthy recipients. He falls in love with a woman who needs a heart transplant and, through a complicated and reality-stretching series of events, gives her his heart. As we walked out of the cinema into the cold air with our eyes still adjusting to the light, my mum spun round and, without hesitation, declared, 'I would give you my heart. If you ever need a heart, it's yours.' She said it with such strength and certainty it scared me a little, and I may have even questioned her sanity. But now, as I watch my kids play, I know exactly where she was coming from. If they ever needed a heart and it was possible for them to have mine, there would be no question or conversation. My heart is theirs; I get it now.

This is the memory that comes to my mind as I read the story of Jochebed's mothering of Moses, how this illustrates God's love shown to us, and how this love should be lived out in these last days through the church. This is no weak, nice-to-have-but-not-essential, pastel-pink-Mother's-Day-card love that's characterized by home-made roasts and cookies. Nor is it a love that traps, entangles and wastes your potential as many Hollywood films portray (and your peers may suggest to you!). No, this love comes with an iron core and an urgent, empowering mission. This love roars and endures.

A divine birth story

> The woman [Jochebed] conceived and bore a son, and when she saw that he was a fine child, she hid him three months.
>
> *(Exod. 2:2)*

When does a rescue plan begin? In Exodus 2, Israel's rescue from the oppressive slavery by Egypt begins with a birth – baby Moses. When we tell our epic stories we don't tend to lay out the background of our character's birth. But the Bible, especially the Old Testament, takes a different approach. God seems to like a birth story. Or perhaps it's that birth itself has a story to tell us?

In Isaiah 42:14, God uses the imagery of birth to explain how he will rescue the Jews in exile in Babylon: 'For a long time I have held my peace; I have kept still and restrained myself; now I will cry out like a woman in labour; I will gasp and pant.' While to the Jewish exiles it may have felt as though God had forgotten them, instead, like a pregnant woman, his passion for them was intensifying, waiting until the time was perfect for them to be released into their new life, waiting until they were ready. How foolish would it be for a newborn to doubt their mother's love because it took nine months for them to be delivered into the world?

God's love is patient and deliberate. In the same way as he has written unconscious rhythms into a woman's body that knows just when to trigger the first contractions of labour, he holds all of history sovereignly in the palms of his hands and his delay often speaks love not abandonment. Jochebed could have questioned the compassion of God to give her a son in a time when all Israelite male babies were to be killed, but God's timing for his rescue is perfect.

Amram and Jochebed, Moses' parents, recognized something special in their son (seeing 'that he was a fine child', Exod. 2:2) and realized that God had a special purpose for Moses (Heb. 11:23). Whether they knew that he would be the one God used to rescue their nation, we can only guess, but it's clear that faith added fuel to their fire of love, encouraging them to hide and protect him at significant risk to themselves for as long as they could. They had faith in God's timing, that he could bring hope even in such a time as this was.

When God's time for rescue arrives, if we go back to Isaiah 42, he suggests it comes like a woman crying out in labour with gasping and panting. Birth hurts, especially before the invention of an epidural. We pant, we cry, we bleed and we tear. Why? Why do women willingly get pregnant knowing the unavoidable distress that will come as a result? We do it for love.

To love is to know pain. The two are inseverable in this life. Just as my heart burns when a child is unkind to mine, or when I remember those I have lost, we cannot love another without knowing hurt when that person suffers or doing something to alleviate it. Love comes with a cost. One of my secondary-school teachers once shared about her son's drug addiction. She said that when he would go missing on the hunt for drugs, she and her husband would search for him. She talked about the great efforts they made to secure help for him. They sacrificed their comfort for his rescue. God knows all about costly love.

As our body bleeds and tears to bring the time-bound earthly life of our children into the world, God's Son willingly bled and tore at the cross to bring new, eternal, spiritual, and eventually physically resurrected life, for all who put their trust in him – regardless of their DNA connection. God's crying, gasping and panting wasn't out of his control as for a pregnant woman. Instead, such is his perfect love for us that he chooses to know the cost of love, and the cost of our sin against his love so that we don't have to. Like a woman pushing hard in labour, he sacrificed so that the life and wellbeing of his beloved children would not be jeopardized, even by their own doing.

The pushing is not all that labour involves. I know many women who live with a little bit (or sometimes a lot) of shame and embarrassment about their postpartum bodies. The hips that never quite go back, the stretchmarks, scars or loose skin (and that's without considering what happens when we jump on a trampoline before our pelvic-floor strength is rebuilt!). Before we rush to yearn for our pre-baby body, let's contemplate the beauty and message in those scars, the love, sacrifice and new life they represent. When our resurrected Lord stood before the disciples, the holes and scars on his hands, feet and side were evidence of the beauty of his love and glory. They were the evidence that convinced Thomas of Jesus' power over death. When my child points out my giant scar, I say, 'It reminds me that you came from me, that our bodies were once one and that my body gave you life. It's a beautiful scar!'

But this story of enduring costly love doesn't make sense without also comprehending the depth of a mother's love. We have all heard tabloid stories of a woman giving birth in the toilets, having been totally unaware she was pregnant (if only my pregnancies were that easy!). They shock and grab our attention because they are completely incomprehensible. From fairly early on in pregnancy, it's hard not to know that you're pregnant. With the nausea and lack of periods, to the squirming movements that prod your bladder and ribs later on, to be pregnant is to some extent to know your child. It is this example of knowing-ness that helps us appreciate the devotedness of God's love for us.

Isaiah 49:15 says, 'Can a woman forget her nursing child, that she should have no compassion on the son of her womb? Even these may forget, yet I will not forget you.' Can a woman forget a child that her body has grown and fed? I know women who have had difficult starts to their mothering journey. I know women who have made the tough decision to give their children away to adoptive parents, and women who have had abortions (and I am in no way endorsing nor judging either). None of these women ever forgot those children. A family friend who is in her eighties aborted a surprise baby when she was in her thirties. She has three healthy grown sons and yet she still talks about that baby. It is possible for a man to father a child and never know, but that lack of connection and knowledge is exceedingly difficult and rare for a woman. However small and short-lived, our parenting comes with an umbilical cord, and it is made of much more than blood vessels.

That is the picture God chooses to draw our attention to when explaining the strength of the connection he has with his people. We are meant to assume that such a mother–child bond can never be fully forgotten, and yet such is the perfection of God's love that it is even stronger than that. Our Father, who created us and knit us together in our mothers' wombs (Ps. 139:13), who created and originally designed the umbilical cord itself, cannot ever forget us.

Interestingly, the word often translated as 'mercy' or 'compassion' in relation to God's character, *ra.chum*, has the same root as the related word, *ra.chem*, which means 'womb'.[3] For example, in Exodus 34:6 when the Lord describes himself as 'The LORD, the LORD, a God merciful [*ra.chum*] and gracious, slow to anger, and abounding in steadfast love and faithfulness.'

My husband, Howard, heard the story of a persecuted believer who once lined up with several Christians with bags over their heads, who were being shot one by one. He was at the end of the line and survived. When asked later, 'What was going through your mind in that moment?' he replied, 'Lord, Son of the living God, have mercy on me. Lord, womb me.' What a beautiful, provocative picture. God's love for us isn't just unbreakable, it wombs us – the ultimate and complete provision of all need, comfort, flourishing and protection for a growing baby.

Unlike our mothers, God loves us from an eternal perspective that existed before our heart first beat and will continue beyond its failing into our resurrected forever body. He loves us with an omnipotent love without end or limitation and out of infinite resource, which means that you are never too much or too little for him to cope with. You will never need more than he can offer. He will not and cannot forget you.

I can almost imagine Jochebed holding her baby boy and hearing him cry, those new-born cries that are like a physical bungy cord for any mother. That's all it took for her to decide to hide him. Some (interestingly, male) commentators have argued she hid Moses and put him in the river because she knew God had a purpose for him. I'm not sure that sits well with me. If you had an idea, and the chances were slim to none for it working but the alternative was certain death of your child, wouldn't you try it anyway? Instead, I would argue that God's message to Jochebed and Amran about Moses gave them faith that there was hope to cling to for their baby boy's future. It was the reassurance to give them peace and courage amid a fearfully dangerous time. I like to think that, just like us at the foot of the cross, Moses didn't need to earn Jochebed's devoted love. His pure existence and primitive need for her was enough.

A nurturing act of hope

> When she could hide him no longer, she took for him a basket made of bulrushes and daubed it with bitumen and pitch.
>
> *(Exod. 2:3a)*

My daughter is nearing the end of primary school and I have been thinking about potential next schools, speaking to experts for wisdom about when to introduce mobile phones, and listening to podcasts about how to manage the coming onslaught of hormones. What am I doing? I am daubing her basket with bitumen and pitch. I am readying that child for the unpredictable, potentially dangerous and uncontrollable waters that I will have to eventually give her up to.

Bitumen and pitch are still used as waterproofing materials today. They would have sealed and strengthened the basket against any water entering to endanger Moses when he was in it. Jochebed was preparing protection for her child ready for when she wouldn't be available anymore. She couldn't control where the basket took him, but she could do all she could to make sure that basket was secure and ready for the water.

Most of us hope to have our children at home with us for far longer than Jochebed, but let them go we all must do at some point. For me, this basket is an image of nurturing protection, comfort and discipleship. We waterproof our children's baskets by teaching them Scripture, godly values, how to discern God's voice and practical wisdom for life. It's teaching them how to budget, how to manage conflict and what, or rather who, to live for.

Every time we expose an idol and take a cultural message captive to reveal the truth and lies that underpin it to our children, we layer on more bitumen and pitch. Like God, represented by the mother bear in Hosea 13:8, who rips open and devours false gods, false teaching and those taken in by them, as if they were lions and wild beasts threatening or consuming her cubs. False idols are far more dangerous than we give them credit with their empty promises. God's love is ferocious to eradicate that deadly infection from his people and church. Now, however ragged I may look after a night with a sick child, I'm not suggesting I am a bear – but show me a mother who hasn't ever roared in protection of her children? Motherhood is not just about cuddles, it's strong, wise, and courageous. Like the image of the mother bear, motherhood is the powerful struggle to preserve and shape the next generation. It's a battle for holiness that God has been seeking for his people since we first ate the forbidden fruit, and it's a battle that speaks not only of justice but of love and protection. In this way, motherhood shows us that love can look strong, it can even look scary and shocking. It can be a bear ripping apart a lion. It can be a man on a cross allowing nails to be driven into his hands and feet.

A releasing act of faith

> She put the child in it and placed it among the reeds by the river bank. And his sister stood at a distance to know what would be done to him.
>
> *(Exod. 2:3b–4)*

I once went white-water rafting down the Nile river and I spent the whole time being terrified of falling out and being eaten alive by crocodiles! But in the Bible rivers can be a symbol of hope rather than fear. God shows Ezekiel a wonderful vision of a river in Ezekiel 47:1–12. This river flows from the altar as a trickle, then an ever-increasing river until it enters the sea and turns it from salt to fresh water. It brings many fishes and continually fruitful trees for food to the banks, with leaves for healing. It's perhaps the same river of the water of life mentioned in Revelation 22:1–2, which flows brightly from the throne of God and the Lamb, and waters trees which bring healing to the nations. This river is a picture of the Holy Spirit and how he brings refreshment and life to us from the Father and the Son.

The Nile will also prove to be a river of life for the Israelites as it brings together Pharaoh's daughter and Moses through God's sovereign work, positioning him to fulfil God's purpose in rescuing his people from slavery in Egypt.

As we release our children to the world, as Jochebed put Moses into the river, we should fervently pray for their protection and flourishing. But we needn't do so with fear because, while the world may not always be kind to them, we're not releasing them to the untameable wind and waves, but to the Almighty to whom the wind and waves listen and obey (Matt. 8:23–7; Luke 8:22–5). As we will explore when we look at the book of Esther, God is always at work even when we can't see what he is doing. Just as he was at work in this narrative to begin a rescue plan for this people, he is at work in our and our children's lives too. Our challenge is not to battle against the tide, but to ensure that we and our children are in the flow of the river of life moving in the direction the Holy Spirit leads us, because his river flows from the throne and altar of God towards hope and life.

Jochebed and Amran heard the whisper of this flow when they gained faith from the special nature and appearance of their boy, so they could release him to the river with hope.

While the arc of progress may be frustratingly long and painfully U-shaped, diving to great depths of suffering before rising,[4] as believers, we live a life that is immovably pulsating towards hope.

A certain rescue

> Now the daughter of Pharaoh came down to bathe at the river, while her young women walked beside the river. She saw the basket among the reeds and sent her servant woman, and she took it. When she opened it, she saw the child, and behold, the baby was crying. She took pity on him and said, 'This is one of the Hebrews' children.' Then his sister said to Pharaoh's daughter, 'Shall I go and call you

a nurse from the Hebrew women to nurse the child for
you?' And Pharaoh's daughter said to her, 'Go.' So the girl
went and called the child's mother.'

(Exod. 2:5–8)

Rescue comes for Moses through community – mother, father, sister and Pharoah's daughter all playing their part.
Interestingly, it started with a biological mother and ended
with an adoptive one. On my wedding day, my dad's
father-of-the-bride speech included a long list of 'thank yous'
to all the family and friends who had helped him and my
mum raise me. As the saying goes, it takes a village to raise a
child. Those who started motherhood without such a support
system will know very acutely just how desperately it is needed
at times. Love finds a fullness in community.

Our Triune God himself loves us with a communal love –
the combined devotion of the Father, Son and Holy Spirit
who have been eternally loving each other and continually
loving us since our creation. As three in one, God's love isn't
selfish or self-seeking, it is perfectly selfless because it comes
from a place of relational omnibenevolence.

As we learn to love as families, there will inevitably be disa-
greement and tension. Community in any form is hard work,
but we are called to it in part because these challenges are part
of our journey of transformation towards Christlikeness. It's
how our love is refined and purified. Community, specifically
family, is the metaphor used to describe God's current rescue
plan for humanity – the church.

In Isaiah 66:7–14 God predicts the sudden growth and development of the church which will span all nations.[5] In doing

so he uses the metaphor of a mother, this time not focusing on his own love but on the love his people, the church, will bring:

'Before she was in labour
    she gave birth;
before her pain came upon her
    she delivered a son.
Who has heard such a thing?
    Who has seen such things?
Shall a land be born in one day?
    Shall a nation be brought forth in one moment?
For as soon as Zion was in labour
    she brought forth her children.
Shall I bring to the point of birth and not cause to bring forth?'
    says the LORD;
'shall I, who cause to bring forth, shut the womb?'
    says your God.

Rejoice with Jerusalem, and be glad for her,
    all you who love her;
rejoice with her in joy,
    all you who mourn over her;
that you may nurse and be satisfied
    from her consoling breast;
that you may drink deeply with delight
    from her glorious abundance.

For thus says the LORD:
'Behold, I will extend peace to her like a river,
    and the glory of the nations like an overflowing stream;
and you shall nurse, you shall be carried upon her hip,

and bounced upon her knees.
As one whom his mother comforts,
   so I will comfort you;
   you shall be comforted in Jerusalem.
You shall see, and your heart shall rejoice;
   your bones shall flourish like the grass;
and the hand of the LORD shall be known to his servants,
   and he shall show his indignation against his enemies.'

This image is of the church as a mother, which is fitting given how Ephesians 5:22–4 likens the husband-and-wife relationship to that between Christ and the church. Naturally it would flow that a multiplying church would be likened to a mother. But the description is much more than the extension of a theological concept. The image of motherhood helps us to understand what the love of the church is designed to be like to its family members: nursed (breast-fed), carried on her hip, bounced on her knees. These are all pictures of nourishment, comfort, delight and fun.

What does Isaiah tell us is the result of a church that models a motherhood-inspired approach to their flock? 'You shall see, and your heart shall rejoice; your bones shall flourish like the grass' (Isa. 66:14). When we bring a nurturing approach to discipleship (avoiding legalistic fault-finding, majoring on encouragement, and correcting with love and humility), the church doesn't just grow in numbers, it also grows in joy and wholeness. Our bones, the essential structure that the church leans on, will be like the grass. Grass can be trampled upon and withstand all sorts of weathers, and still endure and multiply. How do we become a strong and resilient church? Isaiah suggests it's by loving each other as mothers, with the same maternal love God comforts us with. Paul agreed in 1 Thessalonians 2:7–8, where he used the image of a nursing mother as a description of the gentle approach that should be taken in apostolic ministry.

These verses in Isaiah 66 are important because being a 'spiritual mother' can sometimes be added onto motherhood talks like tokenism, an encouraging consolation prize. Nothing could be further from the truth. When we are church to each other, when we disciple young believers, pastorally care for our flock and biblically teach and mentor, we are mothering. This mothering is the layering of bitumen and pitch that prepares and strengthens the church for harvest, to grow and persevere in the great commission to share our gospel hope with others and hold fast to it for ourselves. As the church mothers it brings life, flourishing and joy while revealing the hand of the Lord to his servants.

The great goodbye

> And Pharaoh's daughter said to her, 'Take this child away and nurse him for me, and I will give you your wages.' So the woman took the child and nursed him. When the child grew up, she brought him to Pharaoh's daughter, and he became her son. She named him Moses, 'Because,' she said, 'I drew him out of the water.'
>
> (Exod. 2:9–10)

Jochebed probably didn't get to stay with Moses until he grew to adulthood, and she doesn't seem to live to see him step into God's purposes for his life. At some point, like all parents, she had to say goodbye. It is the goodbye that makes me most anxious about motherhood. As I watched my husband's grandmother struggle with old age before she died or listen to my own mother's anxieties about life, I struggle with the reality that one day I won't be there to help or support my children.

I may roar like a mother bear and bounce them on my knees, but one day my roar will quieten, and my knees will be too sore for bouncing. The roles will slowly reverse as I increasingly need to rely on them for help with quickly evolving technology or for support to climb in and out of the bath. One day, I will run out of breath and my kids will bury me. Sometime later, they'll have a tough day and think, 'I wish my mum was here.' But even though I cannot read nor write that sentence without tears in my eyes, it is not a reason for despair because God, in his perfect love, never weakens nor diminishes. His roar never stops deafening those who would threaten us. His breath knows no limits. His strength is everlasting. He needs nothing from us and so can give unsparingly to all who call on him. His love and presence, which exceeds even that of a nursing mother, will always be available to us, and my children. With him, we and they are never alone and always loved.

Questions for reflection

How do you struggle to know or experience the love of God?

How does the image of motherhood help you understand the depths and strength of God's love?

How are you called to be a mother right now (in church, the home, in work)?

What difference does God's love make to how you want to live?

3

RAHAB

The Decisions that Make Us

Bible study

Read

Joshua 2; Matthew 1:5; Hebrews 11:31; James 2:25

Context

Forty years have passed since the exodus from Egypt, Moses has died, and Joshua is the new leader of the Israelites. God has spoken to Joshua, telling him that it is time to take the land he promised Israel and encouraging him to be 'strong and courageous' (Josh. 1:1-9). Therefore, he sent spies into Jericho to survey the city (Josh. 2:1).

Study and write

- Write a summary outline of what happens in Joshua 2.

- Reading Joshua 2:9-11, how has Rahab come to faith in God? What convinced her?

- How does Hosea 6:6 help enhance our understanding of how Rahab transformed from an Amorite prostitute in Joshua 2:1 to being a wife and mother in the lineage of Jesus (Matt. 1:5)?

Pray and reflect

- How are you thankful for how God has transformed you through his grace?

- Take a moment to thank God and embrace the joy of his forgiveness.

Thoughts on Rahab

We make around thirty-five thousand decisions a day.[1] That's a lot. Some are so small, our brain automatically decides on our behalf, like whether to use the right or left tap to get hot water. But often, our decisions have consequences.

As the story goes, my grandad was very intelligent and got into a good grammar school, but he never told his parents because he was from an impoverished family. Being the middle of twelve children, he thought his parents couldn't afford the uniform and wanted to save them shame (in his eyes). Could that have led him down a different career path? We will never know. Many years later, having worked as an agricultural engineer for a long time, he went to work on a barn roof and decided not to wear a safety harness. It wasn't the first time, but something happened that day and he never came home again. Decisions shape our lives. Life is made up of a series of choices and supposedly each one determines who we will become, as leadership gurus such as John Maxwell would have us believe.[2]

The trouble with decisions is that they can be slippery and hard-won. We agonize over them, regret them, 'what if' them – a job opportunity in another country, a shame-filled sin that we could hide or expose, or the choice to have another child. It can be hard to find peace until some outcome, usually the emergence of material comfort or a reward like a pay rise seems to prove the rightness of the decision. We succumb to me-centred Bible reading, poring over the pages for a scriptural answer to which contraception to use or to which school to send our kids. Sometimes these decisions can cause such stress that we forget what a privilege it is that we get to choose.

Perhaps more commonly, we deliberate many smaller decisions which slowly assemble until we suddenly realize that we've built a life without even realizing how we got there. The choice to keep pursuing one dream means another idea never flies the nest. The decision to pray a little each day doesn't seem like much, but over the years that choice will lay a constant foundation of prayer and faith which will hold you firm against the unforeseen boulders that life will throw at you. After all, a life is made up of how we spend our days, and our days are made up of how we choose to use our hours and minutes. It isn't only the big decisions that direct us.

Our decisions can form the architectural plans of our lives, mysteriously and wonderfully drawn with our own hands but within the boundless power of God's sovereignty and will. But in God's construction company, we can only see the full outline in retrospect.

We see this as we reflect on the life of Rahab – the courageous choice she made to protect the Israelite spies and the grace God showed her. Her trust in the truth and goodness of God enabled her to choose decisions that honoured him even when her future was insecure, and it had a profound impact on how her life panned out. I wonder if God doesn't unveil clear ten-year plans because he is just as interested in how we arrive at our decisions as what decisions we take. God is interested in our being and inner transformation just as much as our doing and outer behaviour. Good discernment in decision-making comes from knowing not just what, but how to think.[3]

It makes me think of Sapphira and her husband Ananias, believers in the early church, who sold a piece of property and gave part of the sum received to the apostles, claiming it was the total. God struck them down dead. We cannot read the passage in Acts 5 to answer how much to give to the church – half,

being good, and we credit ourselves with too much control and power over our lives.

Right decisions vs. righteousness

Making 'right' decisions, like saving for retirement or not experimenting with drugs, is not the same as being good. Neither is doing good works. We all have friends whom we have internally classified as better than us but do the outer elements we fixate on actually make them good? Hebrews 11:6 says, 'And without faith it is impossible to please him, for whoever would draw near to God must believe he exists and that he rewards those who seek him.' God is clear that without faith it's impossible to please him, impossible to find righteousness, whatever decisions we make. If we don't know Christ but try to live as a 'good' Christian, filling our days with charitable works, at the end Jesus will declare, 'I never knew you; depart from me, you workers of lawlessness' (Matt. 7:23). My choice to pursue education (or you could frame it as my privilege to be able to choose to do so) or to have children within marriage can't make me a good person. They don't make me righteous or worthy without Jesus. Rahab's decision to hide the spies was courageous, but it didn't make her worthy. It wasn't what made her acceptable to God or welcome among his people. It was a sign of God at work within her, but it couldn't save her on its own.

Who's really in the driving seat?

Our obsession and stress over our decisions credit us with a lot of control and power. We can forget that while decisions have consequences, those decisions and their consequences do not bind our God. He can choose to leave them with you, or he can choose to turn your life on its head. Proverbs 19:21 warns us that 'Many are the plans in the mind of a man, but it is the purpose of the LORD that will stand.' Our decisions cannot change or knock off course God's will and purpose. We see that again and again in the Bible – Sarah uses Hagar to hurry God's promise of a child, but God still performs a miracle in her, and Isaac not Ishmael begins the Israelite nation. God alone is sovereign. Gloriously, he reigns undeterred by our choices. Equally, sometimes our lives don't feel in our control – they seem overwhelmingly chaotic, and we lament our lack of choice in the decisions we feel forced into; here too, God is at work. As Proverbs 16:33 puts it, 'The lot is cast into the lap, but its every decision is from the LORD.' How reassuring for us!

The only life-defining decision

There is only one decision that defines us. It's not career, marriage, or motherhood. It's the decision to choose God – to put our faith in him and surrender our lives to his care. It's the decision to put God into the driving seat, to say 'yes' when God opens our eyes to see that is where he has always been. This is the only decision that defines our core identity. It is the only decision that makes us good. It's the only decision that can wash away our shame and guilt and leave us as white as snow (Isa. 1:18).

Rahab chose faith in the one true God, and she chose it before she hid the spies. One could argue that it's only when we decide to choose God that we have real freedom to make good decisions. Before we are a slave to sin, trapped in a cycle of guilt and shame and unable to choose what is good and choose God. Once we are reborn through Jesus, we become slaves to righteousness (Rom. 6:18) and the truth sets us free to choose to live for Christ (John 8:32). Every good decision we make as believers glorifies God because it speaks of the freedom Christ has won for us to choose good over evil – and to choose it without the inner sin that corrupts.[4] As the puritan Thomas Brooks puts it, 'Till men have faith in Christ, their best services are but glorious sins.'[5]

Rahab declared, 'for the LORD your God, he is God in the heavens above and on the earth beneath' (Josh. 2:11). She had heard the stories of God's exodus power and put her faith in him, and in hiding the spies she demonstrated her new faith with action as well as words. James 2:25 highlights how Rahab's decision to protect the Israelite spies was evidence of her saving faith; it enabled Rahab to choose to honour God though it came with significant personal risk. Would the spies keep their promise to save her and her family when the city fell? Would the messengers from the king of Jericho find out about her treason? Though her faith was in its infancy, she trusted in God's power and goodness, which is why she hid the spies. Rahab hid them *before* she knew whether she and her family would be safe.

Rahab's decision to trust in God redefines her life. It's transformational. It's what makes her worthy of being included in God's people – not the decision to hide the spies, but the faith that saving the spies evidenced. Rahab was entrenched in the repugnant society of Canaan, living in the walls destined for destruction, and yet in Matthew 1:5 she is placed in the genealogy of Jesus Christ as Salmon's wife and Boaz's mother. Her life could scarcely have changed more. Rahab, a poor prostitute from a nation God despised, raised Boaz – 'a worthy man'

(Ruth 2:1) of character, wealth, position and strength. What a sign of God's favour. She was welcomed into the Israelite community that respected her because they respected God – she was no longer used and abused but treasured as a wife.

It's tempting to see Rahab's turned-around situation and think that she's now 'made it'. But, as we've said before, having a husband or child or elevated social standing doesn't make you worthy before God. It didn't make Rahab good. God elevated Rahab's life, but it was still the simple decision to entrust her life to God that saved her. Only he can make us worthy.

In Rahab's story we see not only God's glory in this moment in history but reminders of his great rescue plan across history – his persistent, blood-stained decision to redeem us back to himself as worthy and righteous, saved for eternity. The scarlet cord that Rahab displays as a sign of her protection is a symbol of the lambs' blood that the Israelites painted across their doorways to protect them from the final plague before the great exodus. It's a reminder that God hears the cries of his people and that when even the way forward seems impossible and blocked by powerful people, God's decisions cannot be thwarted. But this time, in Joshua 2, the rescue has been extended beyond the Israelites, to an Amorite prostitute, foreshadowing the scarlet blood of Jesus that would be shed to rescue all people – starting with the criminal next door to him on the cross.[6] The word 'rope' in Joshua 2:15 means 'cord or rope', but a different Hebrew word is used in verses 18 and 21. This word means 'hope'.[7] Hope of rescue, hope of redemption, hope of our crimson sin being made white as snow – the ultimate decision of our Saviour that triumphed and triumphs over all our wrong and sinful decisions so long as we put our trust in him.

What about the other decisions?

So, if believing in God, and putting our faith in him is our life-defining decision, what about all the other millions of decisions that come after this? What does Rahab's story reveal to us about how we make other decisions, such as what to do about the spies, in light of that defining decision?

We could spend a whole book combing the Bible for wisdom on decision-making and specific topics, but the foundation of it all I think can be found in the verses leading up to Rahab's story: Joshua 1:2–9.

Joshua 1:6–8 – the 'what' of a decision

'What should I do?!' we cry. God tells us:

> [Be] careful to do according to all the law that Moses my servant commanded you. Do not turn from it to the right hand or to the left, that you may have good success wherever you go. This Book of the Law shall not depart from your mouth, but you shall meditate on it day and night, so that you may be careful to do according to all that is written in it. For then you will make your way prosperous, and you will have good success.
>
> *(Josh. 1:6–8)*

Or in the words of Psalm 119:105, 'Your word is a lamp to my feet and a light to my path.' If our trust is in God, then God's word will be our perfect guide in our decisions as we seek to live for him in our many varied contexts. Today, we don't just have the law of Moses, we have the whole Bible – law, grace, cross and all. Will it tell you exactly what to say to the friend who lied to you? No, it will do something better – it will teach you the principles of love, truth, forgiveness, mercy and the power of the tongue so that you can discern how to react not just in this specific situation but in all situations of deceit that come your way. It will teach you what is a priority (inner character, self-less love and the gospel) and what isn't (outer appearance, accumulating wealth and pleasing others) because God wants you to learn how to discern the right decision, not just memorize a list of factual rules. He wants devoted and God-seeking hearts.

What a wonderful truth that we have access to God's living and active word; that he hasn't abandoned us to fumble through life. So, let's read it, and study it to discern who God is, and in doing so, we will discover who we are and how we are to live. Without continued effort to study God's word, we resign ourselves to wasting time, living a partially blind-folded life without any sense of direction or the dangers or joys around us that we're missing.

Rahab studied and pondered what she knew of God, and it allowed her to see with spiritual eyes what surrounded her when the Israelites came. It stopped her from wasting her life like her Canaanite nation and spurred her to action, devotion and obedience to the God who could rescue her.

Joshua 1:2–9 – the 'how to' of a decision

It's one thing to know what to do; it's quite another to act on it. I knew we should give to our church building project, but I hesitated when it came to agreeing on the sum to give. I know that our young children need time with my husband and me, and yet I feel wrecked with guilt when I hold to a boundary over our time by saying 'no' to other people, tasks or opportunities. Joshua 1 doesn't just give us the key to knowing what to do as we live for God; God also tells us how to be obedient to that discerned answer:

> Now therefore arise, go . . . I will not leave you or forsake you. Be strong and courageous, for you shall cause this people to inherit the land that I swore to their fathers to give them. Only be strong and very courageous . . . Be strong and courageous. Do not be frightened, and do not be dismayed, for the LORD your God is with you wherever you go.
>
> *(Josh. 1:2–9)*

Did you also get the feeling God wants us to be brave? Talk about labouring a point!

Immediately following these verses, Joshua commands the Israelites to prepare for the invasion and then, straight afterwards, comes Rahab's narrative. Coincidence? I think not. Strength and courage aren't just for soldiers or leaders; they are asked of all of us. Rahab also had a part to play. Jesus even required it of fishermen. God would also ask us, like Rahab, to live counterculturally, give seemingly irresponsibly, love unconditionally, and to go without knowing exactly where. Choosing to live for God is the ultimate trust exercise.

When I grapple with decisions, I often delay myself with the anxiety that I need more research, more advice and confirmation from elsewhere, but the secret hidden inside is that often I know the answer. It might not make sense to me, but I know it in my gut. I know it because the Holy Spirit is leading me (Rom. 8:14). Instead, what I need is the strength and courage to trust God enough to act on it rather than let my fear manipulate or distort the answer into what I want or a form that removes my discomfort.

How can we be strong and courageous? It's not by our grit and determination but by the knowledge that we don't stand alone. God is always with us. He has made the incredible decision to never leave or forsake us. He strengthens, helps, upholds (Isa. 41:10), restores (1 Pet. 5:10) and protects (2 Thess. 3:3) us as we walk life with him. Strength and courage are part of the very essence of God's character, so when we feel weak or afraid, he will be our strength and our song (Isa. 12:2), because he is always with us. Rahab knew that though she was one relatively insignificant person deciding to commit treason on her dangerous nation, she could be strong and courageous because she was not alone. God was with her, and his strength would be her refuge.

But as we breathe that sigh of relief, it's worth noticing that God's presence doesn't mean inactivity or passivity on our part. God tells Joshua to 'arise, go' and to 'cause this people to inherit the land'. We don't discover the answer to a decision and then rest on our laurels until God brings it about; we are to seek it, claim it and make it happen. We apply for jobs when we decide it's time to move on. We make the effort to get up earlier or make space in our day when we decide to make prayer and Bible study a priority. When we decide we need friendships, we show ourselves as friendly and invite people over for some grub and a chat. Action is part of how we are strong and courageous. Action taken in the context of the wonderfully mysterious truth that God's promises ('the land that I swore to their fathers') cannot be stopped and aren't reliant upon us.

The goodness of God is not just that we get to partner with him in his work through our decisions, but that he doesn't abandon us when we get it wrong. Rahab protected the spies with a lie – the passage offers no ethical perspective on whether this was a deception justified by the context or not. Sometimes we may 'do good' with 'murky' methods. Sometimes we don't even reach that standard. Sometimes we tell the school our kids are sick so that we can book a cheaper term-time holiday (this is illegal in the UK!). Sometimes we tell a needy friend we have plans when actually we just don't want to spend time with them. Sometimes we respond to a flirtation we should have ignored, and sometimes we all-out rebel. Perhaps you can relate to some of those. Perhaps reading them brings memories to mind you'd rather not think about. The goodness of God is that he doesn't define us by these decisions. Instead, through the blood of Jesus, he chooses to see us as righteous: 1 John 1:9 tells us that 'If we confess our sins, he is faithful and just to forgive us our sins and to cleanse us from all unrighteousness'. We all carry bad decisions, and good decisions we never acted on. All we need to do is to bring these in confession to God, and he will cleanse us and remove all shame and guilt that entangle us as a result. Your sin cannot disqualify you from a relationship with God. The only decision that can ever do that is not choosing him. What a freedom that has brought us, to choose and act without fear.

> At an old English parsonage down by the sea,
> It came in the twilight a message to me;
> Its quaint Saxon legend, deeply engraven,
> Hath, it seems to me, teaching from heaven;
> And through the hours the quiet words ring
> Like a low inspiration: 'Do the next thing.'

Many a questioning, many a fear,
Many a doubt, hath its quieting here.
Moment by moment, let down from heaven,
Time, opportunity, and guidance are given.
Fear not tomorrows, child of the King;
Trust them with Jesus: Do the next thing.

Oh! He would have thee daily more free,
Knowing the might of thy royal degree,
Ever in waiting, glad for his call,
Tranquil in chastening, trusting through all.
Comings and goings no turmoil need bring;
His, all the future: do the next thing.

Do it immediately, do it with prayer;
Do it reliantly, casting all care;
Do it with reverence, tracing His hand
Who hath placed it before thee with earnest command.
Stayed on Omnipotence, safe 'neath His wing,
Leave all results, do the next thing.

Looking to Jesus, ever serener,
Working or suffering, be thy demeanor!
In shade of His presence, the rest of His calm,
The light of His countenance live out thy psalm;
Strong in His faithfulness, praise Him and sing.
Then, as He beckons thee, do the next thing.

Minnie E. Paull (also known as Mrs George A. Paull)[8]

Questions for reflection

Think back on your journey of faith; what convinced you to accept Jesus as your Saviour and God as your Heavenly Father?

How are your life and character being transformed by God?

What decisions do you let define your life?

What are the challenges you struggle with in making decisions?

Rahab recognized that God's glory outshone all other authorities and pressures in her life, leading her to put his purposes first. How do you need to embrace the limitlessness of God's glory in your decision-making?

4 RUTH

The Importance of the Ordinary

Bible study

Read
The book of Ruth

Context
The book of Ruth takes place during the time when the judges ruled. This was a time characterized by disobedience and unholiness among God's people.

Study and write
- Summarize the plot to the book of Ruth in a few sentences. Who are the main characters, and what are their roles in the story?

- What do you think are the main themes of this book?

- How is Boaz and Ruth's relationship a metaphor for Christ and the church?

Pray and reflect
- What is your ordinary life comprised of? Let's pray to invite God to guide us in our ordinary activities and see his goodness in our everyday surroundings.

- How has God been kind to you? Praise him for the ways in which his faithfulness has sustained and nourished you.

Thoughts on Ruth

When I started writing this chapter, we were still living in a block of flats in London, and I had fallen out with the building's caretaker over a tumble dryer. To be specific, it was over the late collection of a broken tumble dryer left in our communal hallway (I will force myself to resist telling you all the details of my defence to this crime). The following day my children's school closed due to extreme weather, and I found myself attempting both to home-school and to work in our church's local café – because our flat was terribly insulated and either froze or fried you 50 per cent of the year. Have I bored you yet? This isn't riveting reading, but this is my life.

When this book makes it through to publication, you will see Instagram stories dutifully promoting it with some kind of launch event and fancy graphics, but my life will mainly remain dealing with the aforementioned-type things. When you hold this book and feel its smooth beautiful cover, remember that it was almost entirely written while I sat in my Lego-strewn lounge while consuming copious amounts of salt-and-vinegar crisps, rushing against the clock to get something typed between my working hours and school runs. Writing requires a fair amount of reflective thinking, but most of this happened while walking to collect Vinted packages, in the shower, or weeding the garden. It really wasn't glamorous.

Life, you see, is mostly ordinary, and ordinariness makes up most of life. In fact, our ordinariness is often the bedrock that everything else in life gets built or broken upon. Dramatic career success or horrid moral failures don't tend to appear out of nowhere. Their roots grow in the earth of ordinary life – whether it's the routine decision to do the unseen graft of revision for exams or self-disciplined use of time, or the slow-burn destruction of a thoughtless critical spirit. I don't mean to offend – these won't always be the specific roots of a drama. What I mean to say is that the extraordinary usually grows from how we choose to live out our ordinary, and when it doesn't it's the foundation of our ordinary that usually dictates how we will process and walk through the extraordinary ordeals that life throws at us.

As it turns out, God has a lot of respect and value for the ordinary monotony of life. While the book of Ruth is filled with dramatic ordeals, it's persistent acts of faithfulness, kindness, and perseverance, and the building of ordinary families, that takes centre stage. Essentially, this book is a story about the importance of what can go overlooked or appear unimportant.

The importance of the unimportant

Numerous pastors over the years, including Eugene Peterson, have rallied against the tourist mindset that can grip believers. Pulled towards new shiny experiences or personalities, or even new truths, we can consistently overlook the slow apprenticeship of holiness that God primarily calls us to.[1] While we rush to feel we've *made it*, God leans into the slow ordinary growth of his children, and he doesn't need our holiness to be publicly applauded for it to be worthwhile. We don't need to go viral for him to notice us. In truth, it's often in the humdrum of unanswered prayers that keep being prayed and the hard work that never reaps a reward that we can know God most deeply. We, even within the church, get excited by the dramatic and the big, the multitudes and the extraordinary, but God looks to the heart and values, the holiness behind the actions. That doesn't detract from the awe we should feel at big moves of God, but it should add to the delight we find in the less glamorous acts of faithfulness. *She* might be on preaching tours overseas, but your Father in heaven also saw and celebrated when you responded to your boss's overbearing email with grace and forgiveness. You see, God is less interested in big hitters and much more concerned with deep devotion, and he places no less value on our sincere faithfulness in the small over the big.

Despite the language that we can hear, biblically there is no such thing as 'ordinary' and 'radical' believers. We are all equally called to take up our cross in seemingly radical ways, and to bring stability in seemingly ordinary ones; to embrace our responsibilities and face the daily grind with grace.[2] The challenge to love the customer services assistant whom we have waited an hour to speak to on the phone and who isn't understanding that our lack of Wi-Fi is a crisis, is real. The challenge to be gracious in response to the multitude of stupid questions you get asked by parents when you are a parent rep for your daughter's school class is real. The challenge to watch friends go on exciting holidays you can't afford because you choose to tithe is real. In fact, sometimes it's harder to hear and obey God in these smaller moments because ordinariness can feel frustratingly exhausting, especially when it largely goes unseen and unrecognized. There's no applaud or stage invitation for the fact that I ferried two children to three venues in two hours without a car last week, and that I miraculously managed to stay patient and loving throughout.

The book of Ruth is an antidote when I am tempted to reflect on life with resentment or insignificance. It reminds me that my ordinary life and our pursuit of ordinary holiness is part of God's larger story, and it matters to him. Our 'unimportant' has meaning and beauty to him and can be the bedrock of our own blessing, as well as his purposes. Both Ruth and Naomi walked in faithfulness in different ways, and they demonstrated the ordinary decisions of holiness that can steer us through the most trying of ordeals.

The beginning of the book tells us that this story is set 'In the days when the judges ruled' (Ruth 1:1), around 750 years pre-Christ, when people did what was right in their own eyes according to Judges 21:25. These are dark days for Israel. The people have turned their backs on God, and you get the feeling that the famine that hits Bethlehem is perhaps, as can be the case with famine in the Old Testament, a sign of God's judgement on them. Enter Naomi, with her husband Elimelech and their sons – they believe that the grass is greener on the other side of the fence, and they go to live in Moab. In other words, they're just like everyone else in Israel. They don't trust God's faithfulness to provide and go looking for an easier life in a pagan nation who worshipped a false god that demanded human sacrifice.

But the suffering follows the family, and Naomi loses her husband and two sons anyway, while back in Bethlehem the Lord has come to the Israelites' aid and provided food. Naomi's suffering woke her up to her folly and need to face her disobedience and return home. It woke her up to a life of faithfulness.

Partway back to Bethlehem, Naomi begged her beloved daughters-in-law to return home to Moab. She painted an honestly bleak future ahead for them; as widowed foreigners they would have been among the most vulnerable in Israel's society. Ruth, however, refused and clung to Naomi and uttered the beautiful words, 'Where you go I will go, and where you stay I will stay. Your people will be my people and your God my God. Where you die I will die, and there I will be buried' (Ruth 1:16–17, NIV). She makes a commitment to Naomi possibly even more radical than marriage: she will never return home even if Naomi dies. Why? Because the worship of God is at stake. Moab is not where you want to be if you want to serve and love Yahweh. The suffering forces Ruth into a crossroad experience – a choice between two gods – Chemosh in Moab or Yahweh in Bethlehem. Coming to know God in a place of hardship gave Ruth a freedom to follow his will and released her from the temptations of comfort or pleasing others. It instilled in her a heart of compassion and service, a character so beautiful it later catches Boaz's eye.

This freedom didn't lead Ruth to an easy life, and it wasn't edgy, exciting Christian living that attracted Boaz. Ruth, in obedience to Naomi's suggestion, worked the fields, collecting the grain left behind by the farm labourers. I often see beautiful videos on social media of Christians strolling through meadows in flowing dresses with Bible verses overlaid – this was not Ruth's life of faithfulness. Gleaning was demeaning work. It was hot and dirty, and it left Ruth vulnerable to being taken advantage of by the farm labourers. Without Boaz's generous offer of extra, it wouldn't even have brought her much of a return, just enough to sustain her and Naomi. To those around them, Ruth and Naomi's situation looked like a failed, unfruitful life not to aspire to and yet, to God, they were right on track.

We can still subconsciously read value into people's day-to-day work, but Ruth wasn't demeaned in God's eyes.

In fact, ironically the Bible refers in Job 24:6 to those who know God gleaning from the wicked man's fields. Boaz certainly wasn't wicked, in fact he was a rare shining example of a biblical husband, but the point is that being reduced to gleaning to survive wasn't necessarily a reflection of a person's worth or holiness to God. We see this reflected in the Mosaic law, whereby God built protections in for the poor by requiring that landowners allowed them to gather the grain that remained after the reapers had made a single sweep of the fields, so that they wouldn't be forgotten. In his glorious goodness, poverty is not synonymous with shame in God's eyes but rather kind compassion. Ruth's hardworking poverty didn't devalue or sideline her in God's kingdom; instead it propelled her into significance and the centre of his story. It's her work ethic and kindness to her mother-in-law that made her beautiful to Boaz (Ruth 2:11) and knitted her into Jesus' genealogy. At the beginning of Matthew, we then see her named and honoured (Matt. 5:1); all those long exhausting days sweating in the dust – struggling to do what was right but not easy – mattered, and, in some small way, is part of the gospel faithfulness of God that we enjoy today.

Ruth didn't need to choose Boaz as a husband, as he acknowledges to her in Ruth 3:10. Ruth wasn't an undesirable woman and could have pursued a younger, perhaps even richer, man. By agreeing with Naomi's plan to seek marriage with a relative of Naomi's, a kinsman redeemer, who under the Mosaic law could continue Elimelech's family name, Ruth could secure a future not just for herself but provision and security for Naomi too. This wouldn't have been guaranteed for Naomi with another marriage. Such an arrangement is very unfamiliar to us today, but we have to remember that Ruth and Naomi were navigating a cultural moment where women without a husband or father were in a very economically and socially vulnerable position as provision and heritance tended to run through the male line of succession.

A kinsman redeemer was meant, out of covenant loyalty to the community, to redeem and provide for a widow who had been married to his relative. In light of Naomi's age, her only hope for this security was through Ruth who, in what Boaz describes as her greater kindness (Ruth 3:10), faithfully chooses to put Naomi's family legacy over her own to ensure that Naomi is cared for.

Why did Ruth go to such lengths to be kind and do right by Naomi? Boaz describes her in Ruth 3:11 as a 'worthy woman', which is meant to hyperlink us to Proverbs 31. It's the same Hebrew phrase as used in 'An excellent wife who can find? She is far more precious than jewels' (Prov. 31:10). This passage helps us in exclaiming, 'A woman who fears the LORD is to be praised' (Prov. 31:30). Ruth loves and serves out of a right fear of the Lord and an understanding of the mercy and love she has received from him. A clean fear you can delight in chases all unclean fears away.

As we struggle to self-actualize who we are made to be as women, God doesn't hold out a warrior or queen as the embodiment or shadow of the hypothetical Proverbs 31 woman. He doesn't hold out a homesteader with twelve children either. Instead, he points us to Ruth – a woman who pursued kindness and faithfulness and lived largely within the ordinariness of life with her mother-in-law, son and husband. Ruth who 'dresses herself with strength and makes her arms strong' (Prov. 31:17) and doesn't 'eat the bread of idleness' (Prov. 31:27). 'Strength and dignity are her clothing' (Prov. 31:25) in the face of her difficulty. Ruth 'opens her mouth with wisdom' (Prov. 31:26) as she seeks Naomi's guidance and approaches Boaz; she has kindness not just on her tongue but in her actions towards Naomi too. This is not meant to demean the warriors and queens among us, but to elevate to a par those for whom life is going to be much less seen or 'important'.

God is transforming all of us and we all are invited into his gospel story. All our lives, if lived for him, matter to his mission. In the same way that Jesus came to us as a baby to the family of a carpenter and his young bride, God once again shows us that he doesn't value or need the things the world values and thinks it needs.

Some of us will flourish as women into leaders and world-changers, and some of us will live lives of persevering and surviving like Ruth did. Some of you will spend most of your days caring for others or managing your own limiting health concerns. Some will come to faith in countries where your faith will have to remain a secretly whispered invisible joy. Some will be born into challenging socio-economic circumstances that you will never quite rise out of during your days under the sun. Some of us will spend our days with the capacity to do only what needs to be done – and yet, done for the glory of God, this is beautiful, worthy and exceptionally precious to God. If this is you, you are no less valuable or visible in his sight. You are no less part of his mission. His goodness and blessing are also chasing after you.

In this we see the kindness of God. Ruth is kind to Naomi, but God is kind to them both. Despite the many references to the law in the Bible, this is not a story of the fulfilment of duty. Through the law (the provision for gleaning and a kinsman redeemer), God invites Ruth into an extravagant love story. Boaz wasn't the first kinsman redeemer in line to Naomi, but God makes a way for Ruth to marry the one who would cherish and love her as he himself already did. Boaz didn't just adhere to the letter of the law, he fulfils its spirit too and, in doing so, Ruth and Boaz's relationship points us towards God's desired relationship with all his people.

The law was meant to create in the people of Israel a pattern of life that reflected God's nature. In this way, Boaz didn't just let Naomi glean in his fields, he told his workers to throw extra grain out for her. He invited her to eat with them until satisfied and with leftovers, and then sent her home with an ephah of barley – that's two weeks' supply for two women! Boaz was kind and loved Ruth. She wouldn't just be provided for with him, she would be beloved. In this way God provided for her social and relational, as well as economic, needs. His law, fulfilled fully in Jesus, is meant to paint the picture of an abundantly good husband seeking to redeem his cherished bride, his people.

The ordinariness of ordeal

You don't need to live very long to know that an ordinary life doesn't necessarily mean a peaceful or easy one. Ordeals come to us all. We lose and navigate fracturing throughout all realms of life – family, jobs, friendships, church. We all become uprooted and undone by the seemingly sheer impossibility of thriving at times. Life is as difficult as it is beautiful. If you haven't lived this truth yet, then I'm afraid you will at some point because, however traumatic they may feel, ordeals are an ordinary part of life.

There are many ordeals that arise in the book of Ruth, and yet, while much is made of Ruth's character in the face of them, the book doesn't seem to consider the ordeals themselves as particularly extraordinary. The book starts with famine and the death of a husband and two sons, it then shows us the uprooting of Ruth and her introduction to an unfamiliar and foreign land. Subsequently, Naomi and Ruth face crippling poverty and the vulnerability of Ruth potentially being harassed by men in the fields as they experience the loss of economic and social standing in the local community. These women knew a lot about walking a life of trials and suffering, and yet the book reads as if these events are the background staging to the main story of Ruth and Boaz's character and relationship – rather than the focal point we might be tempted to make them if we were Ruth or Naomi.

Ordeals reveal what makes up our inner core, our deepest foundations, and the truest source of our hope and security. In the same way that we see ordeals handled in the book of Ruth, we can see them as the window-dressing or picture-frame that centres our attention on who or what we really trust. That isn't meant to silver-line the difficulty we face or make light of the weight of hurt that many of us will experience, but rather to reframe lament and grief as an ordinary part of life that needs to be embraced rather than avoided or denied at all costs.

In Ruth 1, Naomi returns to her people full of grief and lament. She feels desperate and full of regret, and she lets it all hang out for everyone to see. Exclaiming that 'the LORD has brought me back empty' (Ruth 1:21) despite Ruth having just declared her loyalty to Naomi even beyond death, she reminds me of my own catastrophizing in the face of loss. Renaming herself 'Mara' (which means bitter) (Prov. 1:20), her words seem wrong and shockingly self-focused because many of us have forgotten how to mourn. We can often hold suffering further away for longer thanks to technology, medical advances and social benefits. Our churches in the West, used to our present freedom of religion, are places of smiling faces, celebration and stories of breakthrough. We jump and dance and sing loudly so often that we can forget that the joy of Jesus' victory doesn't always present itself as happiness. Faith doesn't always sound like positivity. Sometimes, instead, it is the persistent refusal to give up on God and his refusal to give up on us.

We are out of the practice of lamenting. This means when it rears its head, we can mistake it for the absence of God rather than the process of contending our pain with the One who we know has the answers. Lament is not despair, but rather the refusal to settle for the way things are. It is the stubborn, persistent hope that nothing sits outside of God's redemptive power and responsibility.

Even in the most arduous of times, God has not left us, and his goodness has not changed. In Ruth 1:8–21 Naomi gives us a framework of faith in which to place our pain. First, she says to Ruth and Orpah, 'May the LORD *deal kindly* with you' (v. 8). This word is originally *hesed*, meaning 'steadfast love'. We see this word repeated later in the book, and throughout Scripture it is at the centre of God's covenant relationship with his people. Even when our lives feel shattered and full of pain, God's love remains eternally steadfast. Second, Naomi calls God 'the Lord' or 'Yahweh' (v. 8–13); he is still the one true God. Even when our lives seem uncertain and built on shaky ground, God is still sovereign and worthy of all praise. Lastly, she calls him 'God Almighty' (vv. 20–21), translated from 'El Shaddai', meaning 'the mountain one'. This title of God speaks to his trustworthiness, it speaks of the hope of God's protection in times of adversity. Even when life feels as though it's working against us, God is still inviting us into his wings of refuge.

Naomi doesn't just return to Bethlehem out of necessity, she's holding on to faith and, most importantly, these words show that God is holding on to her. Naomi grips onto the handholds God has given her of his faithfulness as she allows her suffering to pull her even more closely to him in recognition of her inability to save herself.

This is in stark contrast to the book of Judges, which the book of Ruth connects itself with from the outset in Ruth 1:1. At the end of Judges, the Benjamite clan don't have enough women for the men and the clan appears to face extinction. Much in the same way, Naomi and Elimelech's family line look set to end due to the lack of a man to redeem Naomi through marriage to Ruth. However, the men of Benjamin don't cling onto those handholds of the memory of God's faithfulness and, instead of walking in godliness and obedience to him, they force a solution of their own corrupt minds' making by hiding in Shiloh and kidnapping dancers from a religious festival to marry. As such, Judges damningly concludes with the phrase, 'In those days there was no king in Israel. Everyone did what was right in his own eyes' (Judg. 21:25). Contrastingly, the book of Ruth goes beyond just the provision of a baby machine as the Benjamites sought, but ends in joy, love and the birth of a king. The last verses outline the genealogy that will run from baby Obed to King David; a man after God's own heart (1 Sam. 3:14). God sees and honours the character of those who love him, and it's with these people, regardless of their status or circumstances, that he will build his kingdom.

God intervenes in Ruth and Naomi's ordeals, and he does so in seemingly the most ordinary ways. There's no miraculous manna from heaven raining down or dramatic plan, but a bond of friendship, a generous farmer, a kind husband, and a new baby. While God does miraculous things, in his kindness, he often intervenes in ways that develop our faith and embroiders the memory of his mercy into the ordinary majority of our life. Each time Ruth eats bread, walks in the fields, sees her husband and hears her son call out, they will forever now be symbols that sing out the goodness of God's kindness to her.

The quest for home

God's answer to Ruth and Naomi's ordeal is the provision of a domestic home. In fact, the whole book of Ruth is in many ways all about the quest for home:[3] from Naomi returning to her people and their land, Ruth joining God's people through her new faith, and Naomi finding a husband for Ruth who would care and provide for her. As the book explores the theme of a domestic 'home' in terms of land, law and relationship, it is also a picture of the story of all humanity longing for home.

What is 'home'? Today we often define it in terms of emotion; 'home is where the heart is' as the phrase goes. Our homes come in all forms, and they don't necessarily encompass solely couples with children. I like how Naomi defines it in Ruth 3:1–2 as a place and relationship that brings rest and wellness. This makes sense to me because we all know of, or have been, people in households that couldn't be described as a home despite the biological or marital bonds between the individuals living there. For instance, we would never call houses that host shameful abuse or neglect, homes.

We all have a longing inside us for home, for a place and relationship of rest and wellness that helps us to feel secure and loved. How is such a home created? We take the bins out, make each other cups of tea, pay the rent and clear out the gutters. We play chess and watch Netflix on cold evenings, wipe kids' noses, and dish out lots of cuddles. We look after others when they're sick and listen to their anxious thoughts. Making a domestic home is a rather ordinary affair and, as in the book of Ruth, it is created in a large part by our communal responsibilities, loyalties and needs. A passionate whirlwind romance, or the radical decision to counter culture through communal living all settle at some point into a day-to-day lifestyle that mostly encompasses these types of unremarkable, mundane things.

When Naomi faced the storms of life, she came home to Bethlehem. When Ruth faced them, she began her quest to build a home with God, among his people. In this way, Ruth's story mimics that of all God's people. As believers we are foreigners in a world still resisting bowing the knee to its Creator, knowing how deeply loved we are by our bridegroom, Jesus, but still waiting to see him face to face. We have a future home with God secured by the down payment of Christ's blood, but for now we still know tears and insecurity. However happy our homes right now, we all recognize a deep longing for deeper rest and connection.

Jesus is our ultimate Boaz, a kinsman redeemer who comes to bring us an eternal beloved home through law and grace.

It's an invitation available to each one of us, no matter how meagre our beginnings. In fact, using Boaz and Ruth as a metaphor for this relationship is an act of mercy as both had a dysfunctional and chequered history of the use of the kinsman redeemer role in their pasts.

In Genesis 19, after Lot's son-in-law dies, his daughter conceals herself to become pregnant by her father, which begins the Moabite nation that Ruth is from. Boaz, likewise, is a descendant of Tamar who, in Genesis 38, tricks her father-in-law into having a child with her when he refuses to let his son be a kinsman redeemer for her. Both of these stories should turn our stomach. The book of Ruth has lexical and factual connotations with these two stories which are meant to make us anxious when we reach Boaz and Ruth's night-time encounter. It's meant to feel like déjà vu. Instead, we find that a worthy woman has met a worthy man and, in God's kindness, they have the opportunity to redeem their history and embody the true spirit and love that the kinsman redeemer role was created for.[4] A true restorative home has been formed not just for these individuals, but for their generational past too.

Whatever our history, redemption is available. So gloriously good is God that, however horrific our past or demeaning our current circumstances, there is rest and wellness awaiting us. It is a place and relationship best described by Boaz as the wings of refuge (Ruth 2:12; 3:9). The answer to all our longings is surprisingly ordinary: it is a home. A new home with a perfect father and bridegroom who loves us 'Like an eagle that stirs up its nest, that flutters over its young, spreading out its wings, catching them, bearing them on its pinions' (Deut. 32:11). That sounds like a divinely ordinary life worth celebrating.

Questions for reflection

How have you seen God's faithfulness in your ordinary life?

How does your faith in God influence how you live your day-to-day life?

Have you known a time when ordinary faithfulness has anchored you through times of ordeal?

What are you most looking forward to when you get your eternal home?

5

ESTHER

Growing Up:
Not Just a Girl Any More

Bible study

Read

The book of Esther

Context

The Babylonian exile happened over 100 hundred years ago. The Jewish people have scattered throughout the Near East, with only some Jews returning to Jerusalem. Esther focuses on the Jewish community living in Susa, a capital city of Persia. Persia's King Ahasuerus reigns over 127 provinces from India to Ethiopia, making him the most powerful man on earth at the time,[1] with an empire encompassing most of the Jewish population.

Study and write

- Summarize the plot of the book of Esther in a few sentences. Who are the main characters, and what are their roles in the story?

- How many times is God explicitly referred to in the book? How do we know that he is active in this story?

- What factors may have influenced Esther's initial reluctance to help the Jews? (Note Esther 1:10–20; 2:10; 3:1–2)

Pray and reflect

- Thank God that he is always at work. In what do you need to trust this truth today?

- Ask God to help you trust him and grow your awareness of the fears and factors that hold you back.

Thoughts on Esther

I've had moments of feeling like 'just a girl' – vulnerable, naive and eager to please. As a student, I worked, saved up and embarked on a trip to volunteer overseas one summer. Like most 19-year-olds, I masked my fragile self-confidence with an illusion of invincibility. However, it was quickly broken as I stood utterly lost and bewildered in an unfamiliar international airport, having thought I'd missed my connecting flight. Panic set in as I considered the limited funds left in my bank account, and tears of frustration flowed as I tried to respond to the giant smiles and empty promises of the airport staff, when a man in his forties strode up to me and said, 'Come with me. I can get you there. Don't worry, let's get you a drink.' So, like any unworldly teenager, I went with the stranger while feverishly praying, 'Please let this guy not be a nut job.' I ordered a coffee, not because I liked it at the time, but because that's what grown-ups drink, isn't it?

You'll be pleased to know that the stranger wasn't a weirdo. He got me on my plane. It even turned out that his ticket was for the seat next to mine, so he was no stranger by the time we landed. I had heard about how he'd sold all his belongings following his divorce to buy an around-the-world ticket and was partway through travelling and hoping to find a new wife. Thankfully for my now-husband, it wasn't me! I talked to him about my faith and studies. I often think it was a God-incidence. Perhaps my words about God had an impact on him, or perhaps the encounter was to remind me that even when I'm shattered by self-doubt and confusion God is still at work. Power doesn't always come with self-belief. I had felt like just a small incapable girl, yet God got me to where I was meant to be and it turned out the forthright man he used was just a boy – hurt, lonely and possibly far more lost than me.

Esther thought she was just a girl; an orphaned Jewish girl, raised and adopted by her cousin Mordecai, living in a foreign land with rising anti-Semitism. A stunning girl whose beauty opened dangerous doors of wealth and prestige with an unpredictable king as a husband. Yet Esther learned what it meant to grow up in God, enabling God to use her to save her Jewish nation.

None of us have a choice about growing old, but it's our choice whether we grow up. It's not just about 'adulting' – paying bills and scheduling our own dental appointments. Growing up means moving on, letting go of what holds us tethered to our immature selves and grasping hold of the God who calls us into the good purposes he has planned for us.

When I wrote this chapter, I was in the middle of doing some untethering myself, because growing up isn't a one-time thing but a constant journey of breaking through new glass ceilings of faith. My fear of rejection was rooted in a series of deep losses as a child but worked out in a prevailing habit of keeping people emotionally distant. It's served me well at times, but when I had two children, a twelve-year marriage and a church ministry supporting my husband, some shattering was needed if I was to grow up into who God had made me and how he wanted me to serve him. It was time to let go and trust my Heavenly Father and his body, my church family. Esther had some fears to untether from too, and through her story of letting go of control and anxiety, we see the glory of God's providence in how he sustained and protected her and her people. Our fears can be a comfort; they protect, excuse, and are often borne out of experience, but God calls us to a different clean and godly fear of himself. This fear builds our trust in him and strengthens our very being – it grows us.

This chapter focuses on three key elements of Esther's growing up into the courageous and capable woman God intended her to be: the 'invisible' God around her; the faithful mentor beside her; and the transformation within her.

The 'invisible' God around her

The book of Esther invites us to trust our lives to a seemingly invisible God. It is one of only two books in the Bible never to mention God directly, yet he is ever present and active, orchestrating a great rescue plan for his people throughout the story. The book is riddled with the most unlikely of coincidences. To highlight two of many: first, Mordecai's unrewarded loyalty in saving the king's life just happened to be read to the king the night that Haman was constructing gallows to kill Mordecai. Why do you think it was that night that the king couldn't sleep? What, or rather who, was keeping him up? Why did the reader start at that point in the records? And second, that Esther, out of thousands of women (of whom I am sure many were beautiful), was the one who pleased the king and became queen just before a plot to exterminate her people began to unfold. Either extraordinarily good luck is at play, or unseen divine powers are working all things together for a purpose. Despite all of Haman's scheming, God's providence continued to quietly prevail for the protection of his people.

Many argue that there is a literary intentionality in the less visible nature of God in this book.[2] After all, isn't this how we often live life? Or at least, isn't that how life often feels? Yes, God can speak directly to us, but such times often punctuate long periods of trying to work out what it means to follow Jesus, in the middle of what can feel like silence and confusion. When work is hard, when our finances are tight, when we're wanting a spouse or a child, and when we face life decisions, the seeming silence can fuel anxiety and a temptation to escape. I'll admit I sometimes daydream about having a husband who's a maths teacher and that we're living a simpler lifestyle on a secluded Scottish island (although hats off to maths teachers and remote islanders, whom I know don't actually have an easy life!). As children, we age and grow under the constant instruction or interruption of a parent or teacher but growing spiritually can be a quieter affair. It requires us to listen before we hear a voice and to act before we know the outcome.

The book of Esther encourages us to join the dots together, using the knowledge we already have of God's character and promises from elsewhere in the Bible to see him at work. David declared,

> Oh, how abundant is your goodness,
>> which you have stored up for those who fear you
> and worked for those who take refuge in you,
>> in the sight of the children of mankind!
> In the cover of your presence you hide them
>> from the plots of men;
> you store them in your shelter from the strife of tongues.
>
> *(Ps. 31:19–20)*

God is our refuge, and no human intrigues can weaken his walls. His faithfulness to his people doesn't waver, and his promise is secure. In Jeremiah, he promised that he had good plans for his people and that David's line would be preserved, even in the face of defeat and exile at the time. As God promised, a decree came allowing the deported Jews back to their land, and the temple was rebuilt (Ezra 1:2–4). He has promised to bless the whole world through this Jewish nation (Gen. 22:8), so he will preserve it. He has parted a sea, sent plagues that nearly toppled an empire and caused miraculous births. Why wouldn't we, the reader, trust that he will do the same now in the book of Esther?

In joining the dots, God also invites us to reflect on our own lives to see the 'coincidences' in the confusion and to be encouraged to see that God is with us. He is never absent. He is the great weaver, putting every thread where he needs it to be to create a tapestry that only he can see, which we will fully know only in eternity.

God holds it all together. What is it that you think you can't live without? God is saying in this narrative that it is himself. That even when you don't see him or choose not to listen to him, he is there, working on your behalf. Allow me to geek out for a moment: if you were to read the book of Esther in its original Hebrew, you would find five acrostics of God's name 'Yahweh' – forwards and backwards. An acrostic is when certain letters in each line form a word, hidden somewhat in the full text. For example, taking the initials of *Holly, Only, Likes, Lemons, Yellow* to make a version of my name (Holly). This is a skilled writing technique that weaves God's name into this story.[3] While we shouldn't put too much emphasis on this point, it encourages us to echo David proclaiming,

Where can I go from your Spirit?
> Where can I flee from your presence?
If I go up to the heavens, you are there;
> if I make my bed in the depths, you are there.
If I rise on the wings of the dawn,
> if I settle on the far side of the sea,
even there your hand will guide me,
> your right hand will hold me fast.
If I say, 'Surely the darkness will hide me,
> and the light become night around me,'
even the darkness will not be dark to you;
> the night will shine like the day
> for darkness is as light with you.

(Ps. 139:7–12, NIV)

Recognizing this truth is one of the first steps to growing up – God is present and working in your life. The act of growing up involves learning to walk on this foundation by faith.

This rich truth contrasts in quite a humorous satirical fashion in the narrative with the powers of the world around Esther, which initially intimidate her so much. King Ahasuerus showcases his power with lavish parties in Esther 1, but it's shown to be empty as he couldn't even persuade his wife to come into his presence. The night Haman prepares the gallows for Mordecai, and recounts the splendour of the riches and promotions coming his way, ends with Haman being ordered by the king to arrange the honouring of Mordecai, and Haman returns home covering his head in mourning (Esth. 5:1–12). We are encouraged to question with whom real power lies, as the impressive greatness of worldly dominance is repeatedly unmasked as a façade.[4] They were really just little boys, immature and weak compared to our Almighty God.

With Mordecai's promptings, Esther grew to see the truth of God's trustworthiness and power. This truth propelled her to stand up for her people. The first thing she did was direct Mordecai to gather all the Jews in Susa to fast, traditionally accompanied by intensive prayer, for three days and nights. When I face a challenge, I often seek encouragement – someone to tell me that I can do it – but Esther knew that she couldn't do this without God. Genuine, lasting motivation doesn't come from puffing ourselves up but by reminding ourselves of the greatness of the God who goes before us. As I grew, I assumed I would become more confident in my ability and more independent, but often the opposite is true. We grow up by realizing our limitations and our inability to be the solution on our own. It's in dependency – dependency on God – that we learn to stand strong. Esther and the Jewish people fasted; they petitioned God because this law to exterminate them couldn't be defeated without his help. They fasted to remind themselves of how great God is and how much he faithfully sustained them already, seemingly invisibly, day by day.

Perhaps you feel as though God is invisible in your story – can I encourage you to look beyond the coincidence that you are reading this message today and join the dots together? God is with you, and he is at work. His name is woven into your life.

The faithful mentor beside her

It was a great kindness of God that Esther had Mordecai. He was devoted to Esther as if she was his own daughter. Once Esther was taken, he would walk in front of the court of the harem every day to learn how she was and what was happening to her (Esth. 2:11). How scary life must have felt for Esther at that point – taken into essentially a brothel training school for 12 months, at the end of which everyone had to sleep with the king. The woman who pleased him the most would be crowned queen. The others would most likely then be destined to stay in the harem, to please the king when he fancied a change from the chosen queen.[5] A shameful life as a mistress to the king or a dangerous life of being a disposable wife. What a future to suddenly have thrust upon you. In marriage, most of us hope the main faithful mentor beside us will be our spouse, but Esther would not have this gift.

We all need a Mordecai. He was more than an adopted father to Esther; he was a mentor and guide in navigating life as a believer in a prejudiced and ungodly culture. He advised her not to disclose her ethnicity, encouraged her, and challenged her when the time came to step into her call to rescue her people. He then helped her bring about the rescue plan. He helped her grow and mature; he saw she wasn't just a girl any more before she saw it for herself. Esther listened to Mordecai, observed his advice and learned from his wisdom.

Who is your Mordecai? Who are the spiritual mothers or fathers in your life? Proverbs 17:17 says, 'A friend loves at all times, and a brother is born for adversity.' Who is the brother or sister that stands with you in times of difficulty? Who are your 'Esthers' to nurture? God knows that we all need someone. This isn't necessarily a formal course; it's a relationship with someone you respect in God. It's looking after your kids together, a quick phone call for some advice, a coffee, and a chat every now and again, and someone with whom you can pray.

Sometimes we need a Mordecai to pull us up to higher ground to see what's being asked of us or offered to us from

God. As C.S. Lewis famously said in *The Weight of Glory*, we have trouble knowing the difference between mud pies and holidays at the sea because, as half-hearted believers, we can struggle to imagine what lies beyond our immediate experience.[6] I have needed trusted mentors to point out when I am being too easily pleased by striving for mud pies rather than Barbados holidays – financial security over generosity, or protective fears over faith-fuelled freedom.

It isn't always easy being a Mordecai – he most likely worked a busy job as an official, and he had to find the time to enquire at the harem every day. It takes time and emotional energy. An ad hoc WhatsApp message doesn't usually quite cut it. We can't be that person for everyone, but Titus 2 is clear that we are meant to be that person for someone or some people.

It isn't always easy having a Mordecai, either. It requires listening and considering their advice before we assume we know best. It takes humility, respect and discernment. But it is essential. It's a vital part of learning and growing as Christians and not becoming stuck as infant believers. We are not called or designed to serve God alone, but to be part of a body that spurs each other on, sharpens each other and loves one another (1 Cor. 12:12–27). Esther could not have rescued her people without Mordecai, and Mordecai couldn't have without Esther. We need to value and seek out the cooperation of other believers.[7] Just like children, we need the help of each other if we are to grow and learn.

The developing beauty within her

Physical beauty is real. It surrounds us in creation and in people too: the Bible describes about 24 people as physically beautiful. It was always intended as a revelation of God's glory, and yet we have turned it into an expression of the false glory of an individual. By equating it with 'goodness' we've turned it into a virtue which God never intended, and as a result our relationship with beauty has become painfully complicated. We destructively limit our beautiful minds and unwittingly pile contempt upon ourselves and others, as we allow insecurity and disappointment at our own created form to take root deep inside our sense of self.

Usually, our cultural ideal of physical beauty is thrust into our faces before we're ready to understand its power or how easily it can distract us from deeper spiritual realities. I remember being at a friend's seventh birthday when her mum commented on how nice my legs were and how lucky my future husband would be. While some of the implication was lost on me at that age, the principle that looking good might help me get places quietly found a little nesting place deep inside me. There is a cultural measuring tape to physical beauty that every woman gets measured up against eventually by classmates, boys, parents or themselves. We all benchmark each other – there have been people I have not pursued a friendship with because, lovely as they are, I deemed myself not in their beauty league to be a viable contender.

Esther would have smashed the measuring-tape test. She was born beautiful, but her real beauty came by growing in character as she learned to walk in obedience and wisdom. Outward beauty helped position Esther, but it wasn't what saved her people. The king had no problem in getting rid of wives that contradicted him, as seen in his murder of Vashti. King Ahasuerus had a harem full of other beautiful women who could replace Esther, and he wasn't even that infatuated with her at the point that Mordecai challenged Esther to speak out for her people. In Esther 4:11 she protested, 'But as for me, I have not been called to come in to the king these thirty days.' Beauty got the king's attention, but it certainly didn't keep it. He'd grown bored with her, and we can assume he was seeking the beauty of others elsewhere. So instead, Esther had to rely on the fundamental virtues God had put within her to win his help. But before she did, she had to break her 'just a girl' mentality.

Esther didn't exactly jump at the chance to save her people. When Mordecai gave her the opportunity in Esther 4, it's the first time we see her not instantly obey Mordecai's promptings and advice. There is a development that happens in Esther's character, more specifically in her obedience to God. To this point, Mordecai's advice has been about helping her, making her very difficult life easier, but now Mordecai comes to her to help others, which has a potentially grave cost. I think we could all relate to that reluctance: I love spending time with people, fellowship is fun for me, but when God asks me to give out of my finances, I start getting cold sweats. However, we must ward off the mindset that what God asks of us will always be comfortable. A crucial part of growing up and maturing is accepting that the end goal isn't our comfort or happiness, but that doesn't mean there isn't joy along the journey.

When Esther first learns of Mordecai coming to her, 'She sent garments to clothe Mordecai, so that he might take off his sackcloth, but he would not accept them' (Esth. 4:4). The sackcloth was traditional clothing worn to express grief in the ancient Near East. Esther may not have known the exact details of the threat to her people, but Mordecai's clothing was no small thing – it shouted out his grief and anguish.

We know from verse 2 that no one was allowed to enter the king's gate in sackcloth. So Mordecai went up to the entrance – as close as he could get away with to make his distress known. If one of my parents turned up at the entrance to my block of flats crying and wearing black, I think I might ask them what was wrong. But Esther doesn't. Esther's initial response is to cover up the problem, to hide it so it might go away. She was deeply distressed, probably for Mordecai and his safety at making a scene.

There are always situations where we choose not to know because knowing would make life too tricky as then we might have to do something, and that something might be more than we're willing to sacrifice. For example, most of us probably don't know the details of how our clothes are made, but we also probably all know that we don't really want to know. Deep down inside, we all know that £20 dress made abroad just can't be done in a way that aligns with God's ethics and love for all people. We are a part of a system that we'd be morally against – but fair-traded clothes are expensive, having significantly fewer clothes means I can't keep up with trends, and buying jeans from apps like Vinted or in charity shops has only led to disappointment.

This example doesn't even compare to the personal risk Esther might have faced. From Mordecai's reserved approach so far, Esther knew that he wouldn't go big like this unless something serious was happening, and she knew that, given her position, he might ask something from her that might entail more than she was willing to risk.

Mordecai didn't accept the clothes. Instead, he asked her to plead to the king on behalf of her people. Mordecai was expecting Esther to grow up – to move beyond a 'me' mindset to a 'we' mindset. He needed her to realize she wasn't the story's centre, that her needs were not the only factors at play. Growing up requires stepping up to our responsibilities and the ability we have to compassionately meet the needs of others.

Her response? She couldn't see beyond the danger to herself; she saw no hope and only death. But Mordecai trusted God's providence – he'd joined the dots and knew there was no way that God would have put Esther where she was at this point without purpose. Like Abraham walking up Mount Moriah with his son Isaac, he knew the future logically looked like sacrificial death for his child, but he also had faith that God would come to the rescue (Heb. 11:17).

The famous line that convinced Esther? It was: 'Who knows whether you have not come to the kingdom for such a time as this?' (Esth. 4:14). That's the moment the dots joined together, and Esther saw beyond the faithful mentor beside her to the God who had always been upholding her. What a change occurred in her when you read on from Esther 4:16 to the end of the book. She took ownership and responsibility for the role that God had given her and engaged her own wisdom – the feasts and approach to her conversation with the king were her own ideas. She suddenly took a more active role in the story; now not only did she listen to Mordecai, but she also directed and advised him – starting with the request to gather the Jews and fast for three days and nights. She suddenly saw the influence God had given her. She wasn't just a girl in a harem anymore. She grew up and into the responsibility and influence God had given her. She wasn't blown around by her emotions but displayed strength and stability. Where did this wisdom come from? Proverbs 1:7 tells us that 'The fear of the LORD is the beginning of knowledge; fools despise wisdom and instruction'. It's Esther's obedience to God and her reverent awe of his undiminishable greatness. In cultivating a right fear of the Lord, all her other fears were calmed and put into their proper perspective as she recognized God as the source of all wisdom. And this is her true beauty.

Trusting the Lord is not just beautiful, it is our journey of growing up. God holds fast to us always, but we must learn over time how to hold fast to him and to let him take the reins so that he can do an inner transformation in us. Jeremiah 17:7–8 (NIV) encourages us that, even in a time of crisis, 'blessed is the one who trusts in the Lord, whose confidence is in him. They will be like a tree planted by the water that sends out its roots by the stream. It does not fear when heat comes; its leaves are always green. It has no worries in a year of drought and never fails to bear fruit.' What keeps your roots out of the stream? What is the apparent cost, or risk, that makes you hesitate to trust in the Lord? Can you look your fear in the eye and trust God?

Obedience. It's not a popular word these days. Even among parents, we prefer feisty, independent or strong. These aren't bad traits, but we shouldn't overlook obedience. One of the most beautiful things to God is a heart that's totally devoted and obedient to him. As A.W. Tozer wrote, 'If we cooperate with Him in loving obedience, God will manifest Himself to us, and that manifestation will be the difference between a nominal Christian life and a life radiant with the light of His face.'[8]

Now you might be sitting here comparing your life to Esther's and thinking, 'This obedience thing doesn't really apply to me. I am not royalty. I don't have the position to save a nation. I'm not an MP or a billionaire CEO.' Yet obedience is what God calls each and every one of us to.

For a while, every Friday evening we read to our kids the book, *Everyone a Child Should Know*[9] – a collection of inspiring Christians from the past. One chapter was about Gladys Aylward – a maid, uneducated, so unimpressive that when she wanted to go to China no mission agency would send her. She was too ordinary. And yet she went and told many people about Jesus as she worked and cared for over a hundred children. When war came, she walked her children for many days through the mountains to get them to safety. God can do extraordinary things with ordinary people.

And yet, many of us won't do extraordinary things in the eyes of this world, and that doesn't make us less beautiful to God, or any less grown up. He values the devotion to him, not the outcome of that devotion. We explore this further in the chapter on Ruth. For now, realize that whatever your circumstances there will be opportunities all around for you to serve God and he delights to use our efforts however small or grand.

A fully obedient Esther proclaimed in Esther 4:16, 'If I perish, I perish.' She placed her life into God's hands. Living the other side of Jesus' death and resurrection, alongside Paul, we can declare, 'For me to live is Christ, and to die is gain' (Phil. 1:21). We can live and serve, adding to his kingdom precious people saved for eternity, or we can die and be with him safe for eternity.

Esther was born beautiful but ordinary, and God raised her up to an extraordinary rank in society. Jesus was extraordinary, seated with God in the heavenly realms, but chose to come to earth and take on ordinariness to do the most incredible thing the world has ever known. Isaiah 53:2 (NIV) prophesied of Jesus, 'He had no beauty or majesty to attract us to him, nothing in his appearance that we should desire him.' And yet, he was most beautiful on the cross, bleeding and dying to save us from the punishment that our sins deserved – the most beautiful act of love and obedience we will ever know.

He didn't need to work hard to convince a king – the king he serves, our Father God, was the one who asked him to rescue us. God didn't need convincing, but we need convincing to receive that rescue, to see him at work around us and put our trust in him. We need to choose to cling to him above everything or everyone else and to grow up by trusting our lives into his hands, knowing that is the best place to be and a beautiful way to let his glory shine through our story.

Questions for reflection

How do you see, or have you seen, God's providence at work in your life?

Where do you struggle to see God at work in your life and the world around you?

Who are your 'Mordecais', to encourage, guide, challenge and teach you? How have they impacted your life so far?

To whom could you be a Mordecai?

How can you cultivate relationships of trust that could lead to Mordecai mentoring?

6

ANNA

Unexpected Endings

Bible study

Read

Luke 2:36-8

Context

Jesus has been born to Mary and Joseph, and they have brought him to the temple in Jerusalem forty days after his birth, according to the law, for purification after birth by making a sin offering (Lev. 13:1-8). Simeon, who has been told by the Holy Spirit that he won't die until he sees the Lord's Christ, is led into the temple by the Spirit and meets baby Jesus. He blesses God, and Mary and Joseph, and says to Mary, 'Behold, this child is appointed for the fall and rising of many in Israel, and for a sign that is opposed (and a sword will pierce through your own soul also), so that thoughts from many hearts may be revealed' (Luke 2:25-35).

Study and write

- What do we know about Anna from this passage?

- What did seeing Jesus as a baby mean to her?

- We are initially introduced to Anna as a 'prophetess' and 'daughter of Phanuel'. Phanuel originates from the Hebrew 'Penuel', which means 'the face or appearance of God'.[1] How do these details about Anna help us understand the significance of baby Jesus in Luke 2?

Pray and reflect

- Think about your life to date and consider the most significant times that God has met with you (in Scripture, prayer or
  through his Spirit).

- Spend some time giving thanks to God that he is a relational, personal God who meets with you.

Thoughts on Anna

The American dream, British silver linings and positive think-ing: we all like to live in a world of possibilities and endless good news stories. We're all striving to live our best life now. But, cushioned by the materialism and individualistic, fake au-thenticity that encompasses our culture in the West, we are of-ten duped into thinking it can be achieved this side of eternity.

Life is full of beginnings. They're exhilarating, albeit some-times pretty fear-inducing. In church, we pause to celebrate children graduating to new schools, weddings, new births, and that Joe Bloggs finally found a new job after his redun-dancy. There is jubilation, as there should be. But deep in the echo chamber of our souls whispers a desperately suppressed truth: this could, and will, all end one day. After all, there is no cure for being human.[2] Our journeys to that unknown last day on this earth, in this not-yet-resurrected body, are inescap-ably seasoned with beginnings and unwanted endings. We'll say goodbye to childhood dreams of being a ninja spy and discover, hopefully gently, that we just don't have the innate ability required to make it as the first solo astronaut to Mars. Some friendships will fade through hurt or distance, and pan-demics or economic crashes will cripple others financially. We will bury people we love and fail to find companions to fill the chasm their loss left in our lives. All these endings feel bitterly, unexpectedly and painfully unjust. Yet there isn't anything un-expected about it at all.

Life's boundaries are undeniably made with paper walls and, at some point, we are all forced to see the fragility that we all live within.[3] Or, in the words of Isaiah 40:6–7, 'A voice says, "Cry!" And I said, "What shall I cry?" All flesh is grass, and all its beauty is like the flower of the field. The grass withers, the flower fades when the breath of the LORD blows on it; surely the people are grass.'

And yet, before the dust can settle on our depression, Isaiah 40:8 bursts forth, 'The grass withers, the flower fades, but the word of our God will stand for ever.' Anna knew and lived this greater truth. It was the part of her that no one and nothing could take away from her. She was no stranger to endings; she had been widowed young, without children and desolate financially. She probably lived at the temple because she has nowhere else to go. Anna didn't accomplish much by the world's standards; she didn't break glass ceilings or raise a new generation. In many ways, her life looked like one passed over, she was one who had missed out. You wouldn't need to sneeze to miss Anna if you passed her on the street. And yet, through her unwanted endings, she learned to cling to God with an enviable faith.

After years of faithful devotion, when her life seemed lacking and unstable, we see Anna included in one of the greatest moments in history: she meets baby Jesus (Luke 2:38). One of the most glorious, anticipated beginnings of all time. A divine rescue that will use one of the most painful endings imaginable – a horrific crucifixion – to fatally trample the devil, the author of all painful endings, and invite us into a victorious beginning in Christ that can never be terminated. A beginning that will culminate in the final conclusion of all painful endings:

> Then I saw a new heaven and a new earth, for the first heaven and the first earth had passed away, and the sea was

no more. And I saw the holy city, new Jerusalem, coming down out of heaven from God, prepared as a bride adorned for her husband. And I heard a loud voice from the throne saying, 'Behold, the dwelling place of God is with man. He will dwell with them, and they will be his people, and God himself will be with them as their God. He will wipe away every tear from their eyes, and death shall be no more, neither shall there be mourning, nor crying, nor pain any more, for the former things have passed away.' And he who was seated on the throne said, 'Behold, I am making all things new.' Also he said, 'Write this down, for these words are trustworthy and true.'

(Rev. 21:1–5)

As we soak up those words with joyful expectancy, we do so while paddling slightly adrift in a sea characterized by the rhythmic waves of beginnings and endings, disappointments and losses. We are still waiting to experience the fullness of this new grace-gifted beginning. Can we find God's glory in these waves? And how do we see this worked out in the narrative of Anna?

Signposts

Meaning is something I have sometimes struggled to find in my unwelcome endings. I think of the Sunday evening my parents turned up on our doorstep to tell me that a loved family member had taken their own life. Or, standing beside the grave as a dear friend's baby was lowered into it. I think of the day I was told that my job was being terminated or when my friend's husband moved out. While we all acknowledge life can be challenging, we are still shocked when confronted with that reality. These endings jar. They feel unnatural, and we often yearn for 'normality' again.

It's as though we instinctively know that the world is not as it should be. These endings feel so unnatural because they are. They aren't just hard; they're not right. Our normal, natural state of being was created by God in the garden of Eden. Our 'normal' is not death, nor mourning, nor pain, nor crying, but in perfect relationship with God and each other. Our losses rub salt into the gaping wound that we are all born with, following the fall; one of our own making. These losses signpost us to the reality of our brokenness and our need to return to the normality for which we were created. Anna saw these signposts; her losses and unfulfilled hopes intensified her waiting for the Messiah as they unwrapped her deep need for God and his rescue. She didn't run from God when confronted with the paper walls of her life but drew closer to him, the source of real power, love and control. She reacted with impassioned worship, prayer and fasting. William Jay, whose work profoundly influenced the well-known, nineteenth-century Baptist, C.H. Spurgeon, suggested that the phrase in Luke 2:37, 'she did not depart from the temple'

> may also include not only the frequency of her actual engagements but the state and frame of her mind. Her spirit there found itself at home, according to the desire of David, 'that I may dwell in the house of the Lord all the days of my life, to behold the beauty of the Lord, and to enquire in his temple.'[4]

I'm conscious that you may read this chapter with the weight of your own endings at the forefront of your mind. My reflections aren't intended to tell you the reason why your engagement ended, peace shattered in your home country, or your company folded, but simply to highlight that these muddy puddles prove to us that it is raining. The whole world is consumed with the rainstorm of our collective sin throughout history; these painful endings are the by-products of a world not as it should be.

I also don't mean to suggest because your struggles have meaning, in that they reveal our need for a rescuer to those around us, that this justifies the pain you have experienced. That this somehow makes what you have experienced ok. I'm not trying to wrap your grief into a tidy package with half-baked silver linings or insensitive proposed purposes that make me feel less uncomfortable about your pain. I do believe that God is sovereign and that all our hurt will be explained and redeemed in eternity. But God is the Omniscient One, not me. He knows the answers to your questions, and I must resist the temptation to unhelpfully echo Job's friends, ignorantly claiming to know the mind of God. Redemption belongs to God, and I will leave it with him, even if it takes until we reach eternity to find out what it is.[5]

God delights in the humble

Anna is like a shooting star. She's beautiful, and old, and she swoops in and off the Bible's pages in the blink of an eye. Like a shooting star, she's made of dust and rock. What makes her beautiful doesn't come from within but an external force that sets her alight. Like Anna, none of us can impress God and, joyfully, we don't need to. Instead, God delights in the humble who recognize that we all, whatever position we have in the rat race of life, come to God with empty hands.

Anna knew her hands were empty but also that God's hands were full and generously welcoming. Because of this, she knew devotion with her Father in heaven that rivalled any husband's companionship; free from the trappings of pride and distractions of earthly success, she heard his voice – and saw what others missed.

She saw Jesus: a tiny baby and bundle of promise. In him, she saw God's salvation plan, and it catapulted her into action, speaking to all the Jews she knew, making Anna the first recorded *Christian* missionary in the Bible. This wouldn't have been a straightforward task. It's one thing to wait generations for a messiah; it's quite another to accept that he has arrived. If your elderly neighbour came to your door today and told you Jesus had returned, how long would it take for you to dismiss her? But such is the glory of this baby that Anna is overwhelmed with praise and compelled to speak this good news.

In God's eyes, Anna didn't lack; her heart had made its home within the refuge of the unlimited Creator and perfect Father. In doing so, she demonstrated the humility that many others lacked. It is a glorious truth that God invites us to partner in his gospel work and that he chooses us not based on our successes or thriving but on our recognition of who he is and who we are not. Jesus came for the lost and sick, not the proud (Mark 2:17). Our endings do not disqualify us, just as our beginnings do not entitle us.

We are not alone

Anna had been waiting. Her tribe, Asher, like the others, had been waiting generations for the Messiah. When she saw baby Jesus, she saw the realized hope that their waiting had not been in vain – God saw them. God had never left them. In Joshua 1:9, God told the Israelites, 'Do not be frightened, and do not be dismayed, for the LORD your God is with you wherever you go.' Anna lived by this principle and now we see that God not only honoured that promise, but he also chose to draw even closer in rescuing us. For those of us who have children, the first moment of meeting our child is unrivalled. We remember it all in intricate detail and with overwhelming emotion. This moment was greater. Anna's Saviour was tangibly breathing in her arms. He wasn't going to act from afar but literally grow and walk beside us in bodily form, shoulder to shoulder, experiencing life with us.

John Flavel wrote, 'As God did not at first choose you because you were high, he will not now forsake you because you are low.'[6] God will never abandon us: 'For I am sure that neither death nor life, nor angels nor rulers, nor things present nor things to come, nor powers, nor height nor depth, nor anything else in all creation, will be able to separate us from the love of God in Christ Jesus our Lord' (Rom. 8:38–9). Instead, God draws closer as a father would to a wounded or rebellious child, whom he longs to comfort and see flourish. However many dead-ends we hit or pits we drag ourselves out from, God is never getting out of the car. He's with us for the whole journey, no matter how badly we, or the people around us, drive. Instead, he leans closer and gently whispers comfort and better directions.

Anna is described as the daughter of Phanuel (Luke 2:36). Phanuel means 'the face of God', a derivative of Peniel – the place Jacob so named after his wrestling with God, 'For I have seen God face to face, and yet my life has been delivered' (Gen. 32:30). This heritage is an introduction to the significance of this encounter.[7] Anna has no doubt wrestled with God through the grief of her unwanted endings and missed beginnings. The Jewish people have wrestled through their impatient waiting, and, indeed, 'the whole creation has been groaning together in the pains of childbirth until now' (Rom. 8:22). Finally, the time has come; they get to see him in the flesh. In seeing him, truly seeing him for who he is, as Anna did, all our lives can be delivered for an eternity with him. An eternity spent, not trying to discern and search for him in a mirror dimly, but face to face and fully known (1 Cor. 13:12).

Saving the best for last

Anna's sweetest season of life came at the end. Rather than 1 Timothy 4:12's encouragement not to despise and disregard younger leaders, often our culture today needs to remember not to despise our older years – that grey hair can be a crown of glory (Prov. 16:31) when accompanied by love, faith, and purity. We are never *past it* in God's eyes, and it is never too late for us to see him at work.

Anna's waiting and ending-wrestling wasn't wasted time. It refined her character and devotion to God so that when Jesus came, she was fired up and ready to become a beginning declarer. The beginning of our return to our natural 'normal' with no death, mourning, pain or crying. The beginning of our sin being fully forgiven, and its power quashed. As 2 Corinthians 5:17 says, 'Therefore, if anyone is in Christ, he is a new creation. The old has passed away; behold, the new has come.' Through Christ, our hope is endlessly unbreakable in the God who never ends.

As we read this, after Christ's ascension, we find ourselves in a new season of waiting – waiting for Jesus to return again and complete this new beginning. As we do, so we may groan and wrestle with unfulfilled dreams and loss, but let's follow Anna's example of allowing our bitter endings to throw us into the arms of our loving Father with fasting and prayer. The description of Anna is echoed in Luke's last words in 24:52–3, describing the disciples after Jesus departed into heaven, 'And they worshipped him and returned to Jerusalem with great joy, and were continually in the temple blessing God.' Let's join them in praising God that we now live in the reality of forgiveness and with the future of eternity.

As you grapple with your unexpected, painful endings, re-member that this life is the short prologue to the real story. The forever story that we were originally made for. A story without end and without pain, where every chapter is better than we can imagine – full of colour and delight and joy. A perfect story which never tires and never reaches a final page.

Questions for reflection

What are the unexpected endings that you have grappled with? How have they affected your relationship with God?

How much of a priority is prayer and fasting in your life – and what benefit could they bring?

How did you first encounter Jesus? What led you to recognize him as your Saviour?

Can you relate to Anna's passionate devotion to God? Is there anything which dulls this – and what could you do about it?

7

THE BLEEDING WOMAN

Blood, Sweat and Tears

Bible study

Read
Matthew 9:20-22; Mark 5:21-36; Luke 8:43-8

Context
Jesus has started his public ministry, preached several times and healed many. His reputation is becoming widely known wherever he travels. This narrative comes before he is rejected by his hometown (Mark 6:1-6) and sends out the twelve apostles to continue his work, taking nothing with them on their journey (Mark 6:7-13). We know nothing about the bleeding woman except this encounter.

Study and write
- Write a summary of what happens during this narrative.

- What characteristics of God do you see demonstrated in the interaction between the bleeding woman and Jesus?

- How does the woman compare to Jairus' daughter, whose narrative her story interrupts? What does this teach us about Jesus?

- How do you imagine this woman's life was changed due to her meeting Jesus this way?

Pray and reflect
- Thank God for how he meets you in your shame with joyful, gentle rescue rather than condemnation.

- Praise him for his unlimited power and ask him to intervene in the areas you need his power to break into.

Thoughts on the bleeding woman

As women our bodies are timepieces.[1] Their physicality can tell a story to the rest of humanity that we often miss in our modern lives in our rush to avoid inconvenience, embarrassment or pain. Our bodies have rhythms and seasons built into them that aren't always easy to navigate but they aren't without purpose or design. It's a bizarre and slightly intrusive concept to think that God knows and cares about our periods and general menstrual wellbeing, but he does, and I am grateful for it. If God can number every hair that grows on my head (Luke 12:7; Matt. 10:30), which I regularly cut without much thought, I want him beside me in one of the most intimate and significant processes my body endures. Women have a profoundly personal and sometimes complicated relationship with menstrual blood. We are deeply familiar with it in a world that often acts as if it doesn't exist.

As young teenagers, we anxiously wait for that first splash of red in our underwear as an intimate signal that our childhood is fading, and our body is beckoning us into a new season of growing independence and responsibility. This season will require more from us than we could ever realize at that first moment. From then on, each month, we wipe, clean, absorb and hope we don't leak. We become experts at stain removal and the silent unwrapping of tampons in public toilets. Some of us become tearful, anxious or angry, and some of us bite our tongue silently through cramps that leave us bent double on the bathroom floor – though we rarely admit it for fear of being the butt of a joke or seen as less than our male peers. For some of us, the blood doesn't come, or at least not often,

and we agonize over what this might mean for our future –
we beg God to make us bleed. For others, the monthly flow
is the cause of grief; our biological clock keeps ticking, and
blood keeps dripping without the joyful pause that allows our
hopes to form into a baby. Then one day, just as it started, it
will stop. With rushes of heat, sleepless nights and anxious
thoughts, our body will beckon us into another season again,
and we will grapple with how much of our feminine identity
we had unconsciously wrapped up in the presence of blood.

The unnamed bleeding woman in the gospels didn't have
a normal period. This poor woman was in a constant state of
menstruation and had been for twelve years, having tirelessly
sought medical help to alleviate the condition without success.
This must have taken a huge toll on her body. We could assume
that she was weak and iron-deficient, among other things. But
it would have taken an even bigger toll on her mentally.

After I had my second child, I returned to work part-time
in a highly professional and corporate environment. I remember sitting in a long meeting in my first week back wearing a
cream dress (yep, you know where I'm going with this). After
the meeting ended and I walked out, a senior partner came,
put her hand on my shoulder, and whispered, 'Pop your coat
on and go to the bathroom.' My heart sank. It was the first
time I'd used a tampon since I finished breast-feeding our son
and my periods restarted. I had misjudged things. A short
while later, I ushered my head of department into a meeting
room, closed the door and said, 'I am going to tell you something that I need your approval to resolve and then I want
you to forget that we ever had this conversation.' I gave two
options – to be allowed to travel home immediately and work
from home for the rest of the day (this was pre-Covid when
home-working was an unusual request), or I needed an hour

off to go to the nearest clothes shop and buy another dress. My period had shunned and shamed me. But it's nothing compared to what this bleeding woman had endured.

The bleeding woman, like all Jews, was still under the requirements of the law, including:

> When a woman has a discharge, and the discharge in her body is blood, she shall be in her menstrual impurity for seven days, and whoever touches her shall be unclean until the evening. And everything on which she lies during her menstrual impurity shall be unclean. Everything also on which she sits shall be unclean. And whoever touches her bed shall wash his clothes and bathe himself in water and be unclean until the evening . . .
>
> If a woman has a discharge of blood for many days, not at the time of her menstrual impurity, or if she has a discharge beyond the time of her impurity, all the days of the discharge she shall continue in uncleanness. As in the days of her impurity, she shall be unclean . . . But if she is cleansed of her discharge, she shall count for herself seven days, and after that she shall be clean. And on the eighth day she shall take two turtle-doves or two pigeons and bring them to the priest, to the entrance of the tent of meeting. And the priest shall use one for a sin offering and the other for a burnt offering. And the priest shall make atonement for her before the LORD for her unclean discharge.
>
> Thus you shall keep the people of Israel separate from their uncleanness, lest they die in their uncleanness by defiling my tabernacle that is in their midst.
>
> *(Leviticus 15:19–31)*

The bleeding woman has been unclean in the eyes of the law for the best part of twelve years, unable to be touched, have sex, or enter the temple to worship or make a sin offering. She had been ostracized from her community and family for around 624 weeks. She wasn't really 'allowed' to be in the crowded street that day in Mark 5 in case she touched someone and made them unclean. She certainly wasn't allowed to touch Jesus' robe – a rabbi's robe. In desperation, she had spent 'all that she had' seeking medical help, which only made the condition worse (Mark 5:26). The loneliness and despair this woman carried in her heart must have been unbearable. This is the desperate point at which we meet her, twelve years in.

Before we delve into the specifics, I want to spend a little bit more time dwelling on blood. Because, while it doesn't make the cut for dinner party conversation, the Bible says quite a lot about it, including menstrual blood. In an age of female empowerment (hooray!), we tend to major on how women can add to and better the world through our minds and intellect. Our danger is that to do this, we sometimes ignore or suppress our physicality, probably protectively, because it has been misused in the past to humiliate or undermine us. But what if our physicality wasn't something to overcome but another asset we bring to the table? What if our menstrual cycle had a purpose besides just having a baby? If not, it seems rather inefficient: a woman will have an average of 450 periods in her lifetime,[2] compared with an average of just 2.4 babies.[3] Only a tiny handful of other mammals in the world (mainly a weird bat) have periods – all others reabsorb their womb linings. What if God created it this way on purpose? The heavens declare the glory of the Lord (Ps. 19:1) – what if our monthly scarlet blood flow does the same?[4] That changes things a bit, doesn't it? What if this regular announcement needs to be heard – not just by women of childbearing age but by all of us?

The message of bleeding

When we read about the law around being clean or unclean in Leviticus, it isn't talking about hygiene but rather about honouring the holiness of God. *Qadosh*, the word used to describe God's holiness, essentially means 'to be distinct, unique and set apart for a purpose'. To become unclean wasn't necessarily to be in sin, but rather to enter a state that didn't fit with God's distinct, unique nature. Looking at this in the context of sexual discharges helps us understand the rules around periods too. Sexual discharges are unique fluids in the body that are holy and sacred because they are associated with the purpose of creating life. God teaches us that life is sacred and that he is the Creator of all life – so when they leak out in a way not associated with that purpose, it makes a person unclean. It's like leaking life fluid. In the same way, a period signals that no egg has been fertilized and made its home in our thickened womb lining, which enables new life. It's also like life fluid. Viewing this with our cultural eyes, I appreciate this sounds odd, but to the Israelites this would have been a symbol of the reality of their mortality and the presence of death that had been with them since the fall in Genesis.[5]

It wasn't always wrong to be unclean (albeit that some uncleanliness was a result of sinful acts), but it was wrong to enter God's presence in that state because, symbolically, a person was bringing death into the presence of the Author of Life. The Jews observed the rules and made sacrifices in an attempt to become clean. The problem was that none of it lasted; more sacrifices were required. People became unclean easily and quickly. Avoiding becoming unclean was quite an effort as it affected not just bad things like leprosy (Lev. 14:1–32) and dampness in houses (Lev. 14:33–53) but good, God-given things such as sex (Lev. 18), food (Lev. 11:1–23), and geckos (Lev. 11:30). It also included, as we have seen, periods and menstrual blood flow. What was the point of all this hard work? It wasn't to make the Jews legalistic or self-righteous or driven by willpower – quite the opposite. It was meant to open their eyes to the pervasive and undeniable nature of the depths of our brokenness, and how marked we are by death, which clings to and corrupts even the most beautiful aspects of God's design. It's intended to make us see just how unlike God's holiness we are. Periods may not be sinful, but the symbol of leaking lifeblood is meant to remind us of why we are unescapably dogged by mortality and death – sin.

Isaiah 64:4 describes sin not like the dreaded disease leprosy, not as the detestable things that swarm on the ground (Lev. 11:41–5), but as menstrual rags. The ESV politely describes these as 'a polluted garment', but the Hebrew word *iddah* literally means 'the bodily fluids from a woman's menstrual cycle'. Period rags. Any woman can attest to the tricky nature of a blood stain. However, I think there's more to this description than the stubborn nature of that reddish-brown patch. What sets period stains against other blood, grease or Sharpie pen stains isn't just that we feel socially weird and disgusted by them, but that it harks back to the very beginning of sin.

Way back in the garden of Eden, Eve and then Adam doubted God's character and ate from the forbidden tree, and sin entered the human race. Consequently, in Genesis 3, God cursed the snake, the woman and the man, but not without hope and a plan for redemption. God promises that the woman's offspring will crush the snake's head, Satan. Throughout the Old Testament, we see physical child-bearing as an essential part of the bringing about of God's rescue plan – God will miraculously enable Sarah to conceive and Esther to protect the Jews against genocide to ensure the lineage to Jesus is maintained; to ensure that his hope of rescue continues until God is ready for it to be fulfilled.[6] In that world, every period was a reminder that the Saviour wasn't yet here; that God's timing was not yet, and their struggle under the consequences of their sin continued. Sin is like a menstrual garment – seemingly impossible to clean, disgusting to smell and behold, and a reminder of the regret and guilt that we live under. To the Jews, it was a sign that hope had not yet come.

Additionally, uncleanliness wasn't isolated to one person. It was something that spread from person to person by touch – sin isn't passive but actively contagious. Eve passed the apple to Adam, who decided to join in. We see that today in mob mentality. We see it when we spend excessive time in bad company and our language starts to become peppered with unsavoury phrases, and our conscience becomes less conscientious when pitted against the opinions of our peers. When someone speaks badly about you behind your back without being challenged, suddenly, that one harsh comment you made about her to a friend pales in comparison in your mind. Your observance of a perceived 'greater' sin going unpunished has persuaded you that your perceived 'lesser' sin is now acceptable. There is no escaping the menstrual rags of our sin. In the Old Testament, the law sought to illustrate this – not just for women, but for men too. A husband couldn't have sex with his wife or even touch her for a time every month. She would be effectively out of action for a week a month regarding cleaning, cooking or other work because everything she touched would become unclean. Periods were a much more public affair before the advent of the pill and tampons. Every month the women had a period, and it announced to her community, 'You are all sinful. You need rescuing!'

How does this connect to the bleeding woman? She didn't have a normal period, remember? Yes, you're right. In my opinion, the bleeding woman more accurately depicts human-kind's spiritual state. You see, the truth is that we're not just unclean once a month. Without Jesus, we are unclean every second of every day. For twelve years, the woman had been ceremonially unclean,[7] but in truth, her heart (like everyone else's) had been unclean for far longer. She had exhausted all her options and was helpless to change her situation, but then Jesus came. Jesus, the ultimate clean one. Jesus who was and is sinless, pure and holy beyond our mind's comprehension.

If we had been disciples with Jesus, we might have been tempted to protect him from people like the bleeding woman, to preserve his purity. But such is the glory of Christ that sin cannot corrupt him like us, his heart is so deeply pure and entwined with the Father's that he didn't need atoning sacri-fices. In fact, powerfully divine, Jesus countered and overcame sin with the contagion of holiness and forgiveness. When he touched an unclean sinner, he didn't become unclean from them like others; instead, the sinner became clean through his touch.[8] Jesus, Emmanuel ('God with us') stepped into our uncleanliness voluntarily and brings not condemnation but wholeness and infectious purity.

It is a foreshadowing of what he would do for all human-kind at the cross when, through his own blood, he created a way for us to be freed from our spiritual and moral uncleanliness forever. At that moment, our period changed from a sign of guilt to a moment of wonder. A trigger each month to glorify God that he came with perfect humanity, full divinity and wonderful love. My period no longer isolates and separates me. It no longer ostracizes and limits me like so many other aspects of the law. Because Jesus paid the price, I can experience my period with grace. It is no longer a sign of a nation longing for the Messiah to be born but a reminder that he was. Many years ago, a woman skipped a period, and her body grew a tiny baby who entered the world fully God and fully human, and he won the victory for eternity over death and sin.

When I started my period, I was told to celebrate this moment because now one day I could have children. Well, it turns out that fertility is a bit more complicated than that. I am sure that some of you know that more keenly than me and have walked the grief-filled journey of longing and hoping. Perhaps you are in that moment now, and the red monthly flow can feel like salt stinging in the wounds of your heart.

Yes, periods can help some of us have children. But as we have explored, they are about more than that. There is a bigger vision to tell our daughter when her periods start. It's one that is full of hope, redemption and the glory of our Saviour, who isn't repelled by our sin and brokenness but instead moves towards us to cleanse and transform with his contagious holiness. Does having to explain that sound odd? Yes, a bit. Will she roll her eyes and be embarrassed? You bet. But then the 'period chat' with your parent(s) is rarely, if ever, a squirm-free affair. I would rather my daughter smirk in embarrassment when I tell her that her period speaks of the goodness and glory of God than tell her a half-baked truth that now maybe, possibly, she can have children, or maybe she will just endure it all for nothing.

One day our periods will stop. The timepiece that is our body will announce that we're getting old(er). That doesn't mean that our worship or significance declines. We have talked a fair bit about the monthly blood flow, and in our culture where we worship at the altar of age-defying face-cream, we can miss the happy purpose of other stages of life. The prime years are the younger years, right? I'm not sure the Bible shares that perspective. Titus 2 is clear that ageing increases your usefulness for ministry in many respects; now you're older, you can help all those younger people who haven't worked out how to spiritually parent yet. The shameful grey hair that we work so hard to keep under the wraps of dye is described as a 'crown of glory' in Proverbs 16:31 (or did you think that was only for men?). Age, when worn by a faithful believer, is something to wear with dignity. If Moses, Abraham and Sarah, Anna, and Elizabeth (mother of John the Baptist) are anything to go by, God loves to use those older in years. Once the arrogance of youth has passed, we're often more receptive and obedient to his voice over our own desires. As we age, how we serve may have to change due to declining health or energy, but we are never past our 'prime' in his eyes because our 'prime' isn't dependent on our stamina, health or age; it's dependent on his power at work within us. He is our prime.

The compassion of Jesus to heal

The narrative of the bleeding woman doesn't just speak about the glory of God's power over sin; it also speaks of the compassion and gentle care of Jesus. The King of the Universe also cares about human physical wellbeing in this temporary body on this temporary earth (1 Cor. 5:1–5) – he heals her medical condition. He raises Jairus' daughter from death and then instructs the parents to make her a meal (Mark 5:43). He cares about our physicality as only a God who has walked the earth alongside us can. Jesus was tempted and experienced physical weakness in the same way we do in his earthly body. He didn't just sympathize with the bleeding woman; he knew what pain felt like, and what it was like to be socially excluded and despised. In time, his experience of pain would far eclipse this woman's experience as he was nailed to the cross.

For this reason – love – when the woman touched his robe, Jesus allowed the event to interrupt his journey to Jairus' dying daughter. He didn't react with distaste or annoyance. This woman was not an inconvenience to him – but instead, he 'immediately turned about' (Mark 5:30), responding with time and grace. The woman and her need were not distasteful to him. It's likely, given the nature of the woman's bleeding, that it would have been evident from her leak-stained clothing.[9] We might have been embarrassed or disgusted by the whole affair. Jesus cared about her physical and social suffering. Jesus didn't treat her differently from any other person because her ceremonial uncleanliness was no more grotesque to him than the moral uncleanliness that every person in that crowd carried in their hearts. In his humanity, Jesus rubbed alongside the sludge of sin constantly; that is why he came to rescue us. We look at his gentle treatment of the woman and see real compassion that went beyond cultural stigmas. Yes, that is true. What is also true is that the compassion he shows when he reaches out to us is no less; without him our sinful hearts are just as ugly – they are just better hidden to the crowd around us.

Furthermore, Jesus doesn't prioritize people and his time according to the worldly importance of the person in front of him. Reading 1 Corinthians 1:27 – 'But God chose what is foolish in the world to shame the wise; God chose what is weak in the world to shame the strong' – it seems very in line with God's character that a woman of such little means and social standing would interrupt Jarius' request, a more prominent and probably wealthier person (Mark 5:22). This woman, like many others in the gospels, seemed to sense that Jesus was for people of every social class.[10] Jesus didn't play politics or people-pleasing games; he was led by love, limitless love that transcends time – a delay to Jairus and his daughter was not a concern.

In our western culture of possibilities and self-belief, it can be helpful to remember that we are created beings and 'human-sized'. By this, I mean that, unlike God, we are limited. Our bodies are fragile, and our emotional resources can run out; we are the created, not the Creator.[11] We're not required to strive to be unlimited but to trust in the one who already is. The bleeding woman knew this very well; it fuelled her desperate, risky decision to join the crowds that day and touch Jesus' robe. Like the man let down on a mat through the broken roof (Luke 5:17–26), she knew if she could only get to Jesus, it would be OK. I want to live with that faith and longing, and I don't want to have to wait until I'm seriously ill to find it. Some of you may be battling ill health now and are well aware of the limited nature of being human. We get a taste of it each month, when our emotions can change, and our bodies feel tired and sore. We experience it when the menopause arrives and reminds us that our days are numbered, and that endings and limits are an intrinsic part of this earthly life. God, however, is not limited, and his emotional resources never run out. His compassion is endless, and no suffering is beyond his power to alleviate. The bleeding woman found healing in Jesus, but she also found an experiential confirmation of her faith that this God–human was gloriously unlimited in power and compassion.

The compassion of Jesus to encourage

The narrative of the bleeding woman encourages us that God will respond to our faith, even when it's rather imperfect. The woman appears to have placed her faith for healing in an object (his garment) rather than in his person. It reminds me of visiting Venice on holiday and viewing the supposed thorns from Jesus' crown on the cross, a frayed corner of his burial cloths and a vial of his mother's milk – all superstitiously and reverently adored by the Catholic churches we visited.

Jesus doesn't wait for her faith to be thoroughly theologically sound. Instead, he encourages and praises her for the faith she does have. This is remarkable because even this sapling faith is evidence of the compassion of God, because he is the source of it. And yet Jesus makes no mention of this when he addresses her. He doesn't demand adoration for the miraculous power that he has displayed, which is the root cause of her healing. Instead, his good glory comes to her gently, in love, as he commends her for the faith that she couldn't have had nor exercised without him. As we hold out our dented, oddly shaped mustard seeds of faith, he won't toss them away but instead offers us the help we need for them to grow into the mighty oaks he longs for us to shelter under. Perhaps by stipulating that '*your* faith has made you well*' (Mark 5:34, my italics), Jesus was gently growing and shaping the woman's faith to see that it was his personal response to her personal faith that cured her, rather than the clothes having any special powers.[12]

This side of eternity, I'm not sure any of us can offer up perfect faith, whether we are beset with doubts, misread a sense of ease as an indication of God's direction, or dilute our faith with a parallel reliance on self, money or comfort. When I came to faith as a young teenager, I went on long walks in the fields near my home to pray and study the Bible. There was a huge old tree in the middle of a sheep field that I used to look at and sometimes sit under. This tree became an image of the unchanging refuge that God was to me. One day, after moving away for university, I discovered the tree had been cut down and, in all honesty, it threw me a little. For a moment, I stood in the field and thought, 'How do I know you are with me now, God? It's changed!' God may have used the tree as a channel to communicate some truths I was thirsty for, but he was never a tree. As it happens, maybe God was in the cutting down of the tree because the severing of my emotional connection to that image helped me find God's unchanging character all around me, even when tossed to and fro by the wild waves of life. I learned that life didn't need to be constant for God to stay present.

I wonder how often people spoke to the bleeding woman during her twelve years of exclusion from society. It would have been hard for her to have had much conversation with those ceremonially clean (remembering this was before the advent of phones and email!). Upon Jesus' searching for the one who touched him, she 'came in fear and trembling' (Mark 5:32), perhaps expecting a reprimand for breaking the Levitical laws.

She 'fell down before him' (Mark 5:33) in awe. How does Jesus respond? The first word said to her following twelve years of suffering and unbearable exclusion is one of intense joyful inclusion – Jesus called her 'Daughter' (Mark 5:34).

Without Jesus, we are like the bleeding woman – continually unworthy to have fellowship with God, cut off from him by our own sin. But through Jesus we are called children of God. Welcomed, not just into a community but into the very heart of his family. Though we still stand before him drenched in scarlet sins like menstrual rags, Jesus stands with us and offers us a covenantal cup of forgiveness – one overflowing with yet more blood (Matt. 27–8). But this blood is his own, which doesn't stain like ours but rather cleanses and washes us white as snow (Isa. 1:18; Ps. 51:7). Like the father of the prodigal son adorning his child with the best robe upon his repentant return (Luke 15:22), when we trust in the blood of Jesus, the cross and resurrection, our stained rags are transformed into 'garments of salvation' and the 'robe of righteousness' (Isa. 61:10).

Jesus goes on from this event to raise Jarius' daughter from the dead. He lovingly calls her 'little girl' (Mark 5:41). This girl was twelve years old – she was a sweet, beloved child with a family that would do anything to help her. She had crowds weeping in distress at her passing. It's easy to understand why Jesus made time for her. I would too. The bleeding woman came to Jesus surrounded by crowds indifferent to her distress. She wasn't a cute child, she had a shameful and distasteful condition, and she had no one to speak on her behalf. Yet Jesus, just as lovingly, called her daughter. As we grow, we never outgrow the need for a saviour or a father, and our God is the perfect Father. Whoever you are, he calls you 'Daughter'.

Questions for reflection

How does shame and isolation manifest in your life? Do you know just how unclean, unholy and in need you are without Jesus?

How does it feel to know that God chooses to call you 'Daughter'? How does that affect your life?

How did you connect with the meaning and significance explored around menstruation? What does it mean to you to know that God sees you in those challenges and is interested even in this aspect of our lives?

⑧ MARY AND MARTHA
Expectations

Bible study

Read
Luke 10:38-42; John 11:1-44; 12:1-8

Context
Jesus has begun his public ministry and is coming close to the time of his arrest and crucifixion. While by modern standards, Jesus hasn't travelled far, his ministry didn't keep him in one place for too long. When he comes to Bethany (a village 2 miles from Jerusalem, John 11:18), he meets Lazarus and his two sisters, Mary and Martha. Jesus forms a friendship with the family (John 11:5), and they support his ministry, especially through hospitality.

Study and write
- What was the reaction Mary had to Jesus in this passage? How receptive was Jesus to this action?

- What are your immediate impressions of Jesus' character having read this narrative?

Pray and reflect
- How easy do you find it to bring your questions, anguish and devotion to Jesus? Ask God to give you the vulnerability to bring your everything to his feet and listen to him.

- Read John 11:5. Imagine it reads: 'Now Jesus loved *your name* and his/her family.' Thank God for the joy and grace of being loved by him.

126

Thoughts on Mary and Martha

How many 'should' statements swim around your mind each day? How many are you navigating right now? Perhaps, even reading this book fits snugly into a 'should' category: to prepare for a home group, to be polite to someone who gave you this as a gift, or even to attempt to make you a better woman (apologies, I probably can't help you with that last one).

Women are experts at expectations. Managing them, reaching them, exceeding them, and completely dive-bombing into utter failure. The 'mental load' of being a woman has gained a lot of attention in recent years, moving from feminist activism to mainstream accepted reality. The argument is that when chores in the household are shared, women often carry the greater weight of the thinking (birthdays, planning meals and chores, etc.) even when both people in a couple work the same hours, which holds women back from having the mental space to pursue other things. Single women will often find themselves more relied upon to arrange family gatherings and look after older parents than their brothers (regardless of their marital status). We can be very adept at emotionally absorbing and taking responsibility for every need around us.

Anyone who has ever watched America Ferrera's amazing monologue in the record-breaking *Barbie* film will have no doubt been tempted to yell at the seemingly impossible and contradictory expectations placed on women. Yet, we can't claim to be solely innocent victims. If we are honest, we also, sometimes manipulatively, place many expectations on each other, and self-destructively high ones on ourselves.

Mary and Martha in Luke 10 are no strangers to expectations – from society, from each other and themselves. They are presented to us at points as a family of two halves: the sister listening to the many and the sister fine-tuned into the 'one thing' (Luke 10:42).

Many things

As believers, we often subtly embrace an additional, complicated layer of religious 'shoulds' to weave into the daily gridlock of expectations: the countless meal rotas we're asked to contribute to for those leaving hospital after a birth or an operation, the guilt as a neighbour tells you that they will be all alone this Christmas as you plan a jolly rumpus with your extended family, and the rota for doing children's work, which stubbornly refuses to be full at any church, ever.

I don't mean to discredit serving God and our communities, which is very important work. However, we can easily slip from being a follower of Jesus into being a follower of emotion as we try to juggle the perceived spiritual and communal expectations. We can spiral into guilt or self-driven activity as we desperately try, and often fail, to demonstrate the spiritual gifts and compassionate love that are supposedly meant to be overflowing out of us to those around – even on rainy, moany, school runs or dispiriting workdays when not crying feels like a more adequate goal. Sometimes I wish there was an award for avoiding exploding with frustration by settling for passive aggressive tones instead: it certainly feels like a victory at the time. It is exhausting and dizzying to jump through all the hoops we think that others have laid out for us, or which we have projected onto our relationship with God.

If I had to distil the chaos in our minds, I would say that there are usually three voices we allow to take residence in our heads: me, 'them' and our – sometimes warped – interpretation of Jesus' job list for us. Without intentional work, they're all always loud and can leave us drowning as they force out any space to wait, listen and respond in peace.

Martha knew all about the 'many things' that can echo in a woman's mind, especially one who loves Jesus. In Luke 10:38, Martha welcomes Jesus into 'her house'. In fact, her name means 'Lady' or 'Mistress' in Aramaic, the female version of 'Lord'; essentially, she is called 'the person in charge'. This seems to fit her personality. She seems to be a woman who takes charge, leads and gets things done. Martha is no wallflower to popular opinion; she has gone against the religious leaders' opinion of Jesus and welcomed him in. In doing so, she has led her household (including her younger sister, Mary) to Jesus' teaching and showed an openness to his message. This passage is not the case of which woman believes in Jesus. Both women seem to have embraced him to some degree. Rather it is a case of how embracing him has impacted their priorities and the voices they live by.

At this time, there was a strong cultural responsibility to show honouring hospitality to guests, which lay primarily on Martha's shoulders as the oldest, and some suggest she was the homeowner too. This is hard for us to get our heads around because, at least in the UK, it's not an expectation or measurement we pay so much attention to. Quite the opposite; I tidied up before a friend came round once and she criticized me for making her feel inferior. To the shock of my Turkish friend, very few of us cater for the parents at kids' parties in the UK. Hospitality, instead, is a smile and the willingness to allow another into a not-quite-clean home with washing drying in the back room. To us, Martha's exuberant hosting seems obviously over the top. To those around Jesus though, their temptation would have been to automatically side with Martha. In a context where not showing good hospitality brought shame, Martha was the one to be imitated.

In fact, Jesus himself had just elevated the act of compassionate hospitality in the parable of the good Samaritan that comes immediately before this passage in Luke, and Scripture holds hospitality in high regard throughout the Bible. Martha wasn't doing anything that was wrong, but rather how and why she was doing it had missed the point. No one enjoyed her hospitality and welcome more than Jesus, but his tired body and human need for her serving couldn't distract him from the real issues of Martha's heart.[1] His love wouldn't let them go unaddressed because he knew that he was the answer to quietening the noise of expectations in her mind that was driving her intense activity.

The 'much serving' (Luke 10:40) phrase used in Jesus' comment shows an over-exuberance in Martha's efforts that went beyond what was necessary. One could, as Judas did, make the same criticism of Mary in John 12 when she used expensive perfume, worth a year's wages (and possibly her dowry), to wash Jesus' feet. However, Martha's attitude accompanying this lavish show of hospitality seems different from Mary's.

Martha is resentful at her sister's absence from the kitchen. Emboldened by stress, Martha is rude and arrogant in her rebuke of Jesus for allowing Mary to sit and listen to him instead. In fact, Martha's rebuke has echoes of Judas Iscariot's words from John 12. Judas stated that Mary was wasting the perfume, and it could be better used elsewhere (even though he was stealing from the money bags), and Martha thought Mary was wasting her time at Jesus' feet and that her efforts could be better used in the kitchen with her. Judas was twisted by an unmet and misguided expectation that Jesus would be an earthly warrior king who would bring him and the Jews power and dominion in the immediate worldly sense. Martha had slipped into thinking that Jesus expected or needed something extraordinary from her. The cultural pressure she had absorbed – to provide hospitality to match the honour that her guest, the King of the Universe, deserved – felt immense.

It reminds me of the parable of the seeds in Luke 8 and the seed that falls among the thorns. The believer receives the gospel and believes, but over time the young plant is choked by the cares of life (Luke 8:4–14). Martha, in focusing on the many things and much serving, became 'distracted' (Luke 10:40) after inviting Jesus into her home and, instead of focusing on the one thing necessary, was consumed with personal and cultural cares and expectations.

When life, or even faith, feels difficult, we can default to many things: to-do lists, new Bible reading plans or structures to our day, another job or study opportunity . . . the list goes on. We pull other people in to help us manage our overwhelming workloads or the logistical tightropes we walk between our many commitments. When Martha asked for 'help' she used the Greek word, *sunantilambanomai*. This word is used only twice in the Bible. The other time it is used is in Romans 8:26 when Paul promises that the Holy Spirit will 'help' us.[2] When we cry out under pressure, the only help that can meet our need comes from God. We often have a set idea of what the help we need looks like, but God has a perfect understanding of our true need, and his help can often seem a little left-field.

Martha thought she needed a sister in the kitchen with her to complete the cooking, but God knew Martha actually needed to get out of the kitchen, lay down the distracting expectations keeping her like a hamster in a wheel, and do the one thing necessary – listen to Jesus. Put the feast to one side, just bring out some bread, butter and olives and come, listen to his voice. It is the only one that you need to hear. It's the only effective help and it's the only expectation he has of us; listen and be changed.

One thing

In contrast to the 'many things' that the world asks of us, and the 'much serving' we imagine is needed, God's gentle goodness is shown through Jesus' response to Martha's anxiety: 'but one thing is necessary. Mary has chosen the good portion, which will not be taken away from her' (Luke 10:42).

God doesn't want many things from us. Rather than demanding more, he asks for less. There is just one necessary thing he asks for: come to me. Come to Jesus, listen and respond. In Matthew 11:28–30 (NIV), Jesus said, 'Come to me, all you who are weary and burdened, and I will give you rest. Take my yoke upon you and learn from me, for I am gentle and humble in heart, and you will find rest for your souls. For my yoke is easy and my burden is light.' We are not meant to be left dizzy or drowning under God's expectations of us. Instead, his request brings us rest and release, refreshment and liberation. God may have plans for us, but he doesn't have a never-ending job list that exhausts and crushes joy.

A yoke is a wooden beam used between animals, usually oxen, to enable them to pull a load together. It was an essential piece of farming equipment in biblical times used to tend to the land. There is work for us to do together as a people of God as we steward the earth and share the good news: harvesting souls for him. But Jesus brings us rest and ease in that work by asking us to focus on just one thing – himself. In doing so we find freedom and peace of mind as the voices simplify into one low whisper of love (1 Kgs 19:11–13). We see this lived out in Mary.

In every passage in which we encounter Mary, she is at or falls at Jesus' feet. It demonstrates a lifestyle and attitude of worship and reverence, and the overflow of being fully known and loved. It enabled her to show lavish devotion to Jesus in John 12 without the condemnation of Judas or the guilt of the needy poor distracting her. It shows us how listening to Jesus brings clarity and freedom from anxiety.

The relationship Jesus invites us to isn't one-way. It's a reciprocal friendship. As Mary listened to Jesus, Jesus was listening to Martha. Martha's mind was distracted from Jesus by her work in the kitchen, but Jesus' mind cannot be distracted from us even when he is in the middle of his own work. Instead, while teaching Mary, he heard Martha's heart (and probably her body language and tone of voice too). When he replied to Martha, he didn't address the issue of hospitality and how much kitchen work was required from Mary, instead he went straight to Martha's point of need because he knew and heard her. He heard the voices of expectation she had piled upon herself and imagined from others. He listened to her anxious thoughts and busybodying. So he responded by addressing her anxiety and dispelling the expectations that were guiding her.

Jesus softly rebukes Martha and indirectly invites her to join Mary in 'the good portion' (Luke 10:42). He invites her to lay down the spatula, rest and listen to him. The image of 'portion' has significance in the Old Testament particularly. Psalm 16:5–6 says 'The LORD is my chosen portion and my cup; you hold my lot. The lines have fallen for me in pleasant places; indeed, I have a beautiful inheritance.' Jesus is reminding Martha gently that when she rants at him, she is speaking face to face with God, and he is God without burdensome demands but with a rich and pleasant inheritance.

That portion isn't a contractual inheritance, but a relational one. Jesus loved Martha, Mary and their brother Lazarus (John 11:5), not just as followers but as friends. He spent time with them, cared for them deeply and grieved at the loss of Lazarus when he died, and the pain Mary and Martha endured through that loss.

In reflecting on the theme of friendship with Jesus, Ian Galloway argues that to know another person we have to know many stories about them and see their behaviour played out so that we can learn their patterns of behaviour and understand them. He draws our attention to how we see this in John's biography here, in how it mimics the narratives of 2 Kings 4–5. When we get to the account of Mary and Martha seeing Jesus call Lazarus back to life, Galloway finds sixteen points of correspondence between this narrative and that of Elisha and the raising of the Shunammite's son.

In fact, he finds in both John's Gospel and 2 Kings 4–5 a run of four corresponding stories: one where reality is changed by the pouring in and out of jars (John 2:1–12; 2 Kgs 4:1–7), healing by walking away (John 4:43–54; 2 Kgs 5:1–19), bread multiplying to feed people (John 6:1–21; 2 Kgs 4:42–4), and a beloved dead son of a family being brought back to life (John 10:40 – 11:54; 2 Kgs 4:8–37). He points out that by mimicking this rhythm of narrative, God, through John, has intentionally written the story of Jesus within the story of Israel.[3] This not only points towards Jesus being the Saviour and the Word made flesh, but also makes friendship with Jesus more accessible as we see the consistency of God's goodness played out in corresponding narratives.[4] This is a gift to us today. Mary and Martha might have caught the similarities as they lived it out, but this is a literary technique primarily for us, post-ascension, who largely find friendship with Jesus through his written word, the Bible. It helps us to trust him when we don't get to hear his tone of voice, see his body language, or touch his embrace. It helps us to see the beauty of this 'good portion' and the space that is still available for us at his feet.

More things

My daughter is a keen gymnast and I have often joked that she cartwheels more than she walks. Slowly, gymnastics has encroached on all the rooms in our house: we have a foldable gym beam in our lounge and a high gym bar inconveniently located in the kitchen doorway. It feels as though she is always upside down or spinning over something as we all run for cover to protect our faces from flailing legs. She is all-out committed because she's been taught that hard work produces good results. Her coach drills into her the principle that the more you put in, the more you'll get back. Practice makes perfect, as the saying goes. Essentially, more, brings more. But Jesus, having called us away from the many things to the one necessary thing (himself; listening to him and responding), leaves us not with less but with abundance.

Jesus described himself to Martha as 'the good portion' (Luke 10:42). In John 11, where Jesus raises her brother, Lazarus, from the dead, we find out just how abundantly good and unlimited that portion and inheritance is.

When Jesus is told of Lazarus' illness, he intentionally delays before going to help. In contrast to Martha's frenzied, urgent activity to do many things, Jesus is deliberate and thoughtful. He takes his time and acts in response to the Holy Spirit and his Father's desire, not anxiety.

By delaying two days, Jesus arrived four days after Lazarus had died (John 11:17). This is significant because Jewish thinking at the time was that the soul remained in the body for three days after death.[5] So by day four, Lazarus was utterly gone. To Martha, Mary and those around, it was now truly beyond hope.

Why did Jesus wait until this moment? In John 11:4, when Jesus first learns of Lazarus' illness, he knows through the Holy Spirit that this illness won't lead to death but 'it is for the glory of God'. Then verses 5 to 6 suggest that he delays out of love for Martha, Mary and Lazarus. Jesus slows down, listens to his Father and intentionally acts to do the necessary, rather than the distracted many things, so that God's glory will be revealed in even greater measure. In this way, the friends he dearly loved could experience the awe of seeing an even greater measure of God's glory. You could say that this delay speaks of the generosity of Jesus' friendship by sharing such glorious glimpses of the Father's goodness and power with us.

Both Mary and Martha greeted Jesus in John 11 saying, 'if you had been here' (vv. 21,32). They had faith that he could heal, but not now that Lazarus' soul had departed. Not now that his body had started decomposing. Yet Jesus shows us that we can expect more from him than we could ever imagine. He wants us to listen and focus on the necessary things, so that he can invite us into an experience of more things. He is more powerful, more loving, more generous.

We see this even more clearly when we look at the context of this narrative. Immediately before, in John 10, Jesus has been teaching about being the good shepherd and he and his father being one. He spoke of laying down his own life for his sheep and in John 10:27–8 he says, 'My sheep hear my voice, and I know them, and they follow me. I give them eternal life, and they will never perish, and no one will snatch them out of my hand.' When we get to John 11 with Mary and Martha, we then see a working out of this teaching in this miracle. Jesus calls out to Lazarus, Lazarus hears his voice (even though he was dead, as we sheep are spiritually dead without Jesus) and follows him out into life again. Jesus then commands, 'Unbind him, and let him go' (John 11:44), free from death, as we sheep responding to his voice can walk out of spiritual death and throw off the sin that entangles us (Heb. 12:1–3).

I can imagine sitting at Jesus' feet as he taught about being the good shepherd and thinking that I understood what he was saying. Perhaps even thinking that, by listening to his teaching and following him as a rabbi, I was already living it out as a sheep that was responding to my good shepherd. Jesus brings transformation through teaching, but he wants us to know that there is more that he can do than teach. When Mary and Martha exclaimed, 'If you had only been here', they were right to believe that Jesus can heal as he has done many times up to this point in the gospels. But Jesus can do more than just heal. Had Jesus immediately left upon news of Lazarus' illness, he still would have arrived after he died, and he could have raised him, freshly deceased, as he did with Jarius' little girl (Matt. 9:23–5). But Jesus can do more than raise the dead. Instead, Jesus, the good shepherd, gives life to the most lost a sheep could ever be. Lazarus wasn't just dead; at four days dead, he was soulless. Physically and spiritually lost to all help. This is who Jesus called out of the tomb. It is who he still calls out to; those lost to physical and spiritual death whom no one or nothing else can help. Jesus truly is the good shepherd who is the door to abundant eternal life even for the most lost sheep. He can free us from the cords of sin (Prov. 5:22) that bind us, and free us from death forever. He is beyond our wildest expectations.

Jesus doesn't just have power over physical death, but over our spiritual death. He can breathe life into our very souls. He isn't just king over the universe we see before us, but he even has victory over all that lies beyond that. All that we don't see and can't really understand – such as the space once our soul has departed. We can expect more things from Jesus than we can imagine. Just as we think we know him he surprises us with more. There is always more: more power, more goodness, more glory.

Before Jesus raised Lazarus from the dead, he wept. Power and divinity don't mean being free from pain and sorrows. Knowing that resurrection is to come doesn't take away the grief of loss right now. It didn't for Jesus either – he was 'a man of sorrows, and acquainted with grief' (Isa. 53:3) because he didn't just do miracles, he deeply loved people. When we see this narrative layered over the teaching of the good shepherd, we can see that his grief isn't just for his friend, Lazarus. This miracle is the story of the death and decay that we all live in. We may go to work, drink our lattes with friends and enjoy holidays, but we are all Lazarus without Jesus. We are spiritually dead, and a permanent physical death is always lingering at some unknown point in the future. Our lives now are punctured with profound loss and difficulty. Jesus wept and still weeps at the wreckage that sin makes in all our lives. As he wept for his friends, he also wept for all of us.

Such is his grief and love that he would choose to take that sin upon himself to bring us freedom and release. This resurrection of Lazarus was the final tipping point for the chief priests and Pharisees who then plotted to kill Jesus. This wasn't an unfortunate turn of events, but an intentional choice of Jesus to willingly give over the very thing he had just gifted to Lazarus – his life. In John 10:18, Jesus taught in relation to his own life that 'No one takes it from me, but I lay it down of my own accord. I have authority to lay it down, and I have authority to take it up again. This charge I have received from my Father.' This plot only succeeds, because the Father has allowed it, and Jesus has chosen it.

In beholding the cross, we see even more things. We see that Jesus can't just raise the soulless, physically, and the spiritually dead to life; he can and did do it at the cost of his own. He didn't just die. Instead, on the third day that the Jews believed his soul would depart from his lifeless body, Jesus took his life back up again and in doing so he saved the souls of every sheep that would ever hear and know his voice. One day we can all be Lazarus, walking out of the tomb into Jesus' arms. One day we can all be Mary and Martha, watching our brothers and sisters rejoin us in life – but this time it will be life for ever.

We can expect more things from Jesus as we expect fewer things from ourselves. When we lay aside the frazzled juggling, we find a generous friend in Jesus who has one simple expectation of us: listen and respond. His is the only voice we need to listen to, and it brings help that meets our real needs with rest, life and abundant hope.

O Love divine, how sweet Thou art

Oh, that I could forever sit
Like Mary, at the Master's feet;
   Be this my happy choice;
My only care, delight, and bliss,
My joy, my rest on earth be this,
   To hear the bridegroom's voice.

Charles Wesley, 1759

Questions for reflection

What are the external voices and internal anxiety that you struggle with?

How are you distracted from being at Jesus' feet? How could you bring yourself back to this place again?

What difference would living for God's voice above all others make to your life right now?

What aspect of God's glory are you in awe of today?

9 THE WOMAN AT THE WELL

Finding True Love

By Howard Satterthwaite

Bible study

Read

John 4:1–42

Context

Jesus is in the early part of his ministry. He's called his first disciples. He's turned water into wine. He's cleansed the temple, and he's discussed the necessity of new birth with Nicodemus. Now he travels to Sychar in Samaria.

Study and write

- What does Jesus say and do that helps this unnamed woman come to know him? What, if anything, is surprising about this?

- What evidence is there in the passage that this woman is transformed by Jesus? How do you explain this change?

Pray and reflect

- Thank God that he wants to sit and converse with you, no matter how ashamed you may feel, or shameful you are.

- Ask God to help you to open up to him and share the things you're most embarrassed and ashamed of.

Thoughts on the woman at the well

Every human being has an ache they cannot shake. It's a cliché called the God-shaped hole in your soul: that insatiable inner itch nothing in this world can fully comfort or fix. It is, as the chapter title suggests, about our longing for love.

People have looked for it in all sorts of ways (Tinder, *Love Island*, and that sideways glance at the guy or girl who's always on your bus) and in all kinds of places (holidays in Ibiza, speed-dating events and every church youth group that you've ever attended). Hollywood and its rom-com industry love to keep spinning their 'you're incomplete without your special other half' messaging, and we continuously flock to hear it. Social media is overrun each Christmas with images of people 'getting into the spirit of Christmas' with *The Holiday* and *Love Actually*. It seems that, to the world, to be truly loved requires finding someone who's our perfect fit, a soul mate who needs us as much as we need them. Ideally, they'll also like children and, my wife tells me, they'll remember to put the toilet seat down.

I've known many who feel stuck in life trying to desperately find 'the one', often experiencing the agony of unrequited love, rejection and even betrayal. In a world that so often seems built for couples, particularly in some 'Christian' contexts, this can awaken or compound our 'I'm not good enough' shame narratives that spiral inside our minds. But even those who think they've found 'true love' still feel somewhat empty inside. As Holly's husband, can I honestly say that I complete her? It would be foolish to think that either of us could ever complete that which we didn't create – and provide the fullness of love that each of our God-shaped souls craves. Perhaps this is why many marriages start well but, several years later, people say they've 'fallen out of love with each other'. Dissatisfaction and resentment grow when we set impossible expectations for each other to meet. We can sometimes fall into viewing love as some kind of cosmic force that's outside of our control, like Cupid's arrow, yet love is surely more about devotion than emotion. Isn't the power of love based on the choice to love, come what may?

Admittedly I'm not telling you anything you probably don't already know. But I do want to set the scene for the woman at the well, and her love-stuck personal turmoil. At the hottest point of the day, when most people would be staying cool in the shade, or taking a siesta, she was collecting water on her own, which was something women typically did together. They didn't want to be with her, and she probably didn't want to be with them. Why? Because of the shame of her relationship history.

Shame conveys a deep sense of personal inadequacy, making us feel inherently flawed and worthless. It embodies a negative self-narrative, often leading to the belief you'll inevitably fall short in crucial moments. Psychiatrist Curt Thompson highlights that shame is a fundamental tool of evil, giving rise to various forms of wrongdoing. Its strength lies in its subtlety and silence, acting as a primal barrier to personal growth and flourishing. Thompson likens shame to carbon, an essential element found in all living organisms, underscoring its pervasive presence in human experience.[1] Everyone has shame; it's just that some are more aware of how it affects them than others.

What was the cause of the Samaritan woman's shame? In short, she'd been married five times, and the man she was currently living with and most likely sleeping with was not her husband. People have seen her as everything, from a sexually immoral flirtatious woman to a bereaved widow (noting the historically higher mortality rate of men) and/or a victim of cruel men who could have divorced her for next to no reason whatsoever. Some rabbis in first-century Palestine taught that a man had a perfect right to divorce his wife if he found another woman whom he liked better or was more 'beautiful' (Mishnah, Gittin, 14 10):

> The following women may be divorced: She who violates the Law of Moses, e.g. causes her husband to eat food which has not been tithed . . . She who vows, but does not keep her vows . . . She who goes out on the street with her hair loose, or spins in the street, or converses [flirts] with any man, or is a noisy woman. What is a noisy woman? It is one who speaks in her own house so loud that the neighbours may hear her.
>
> *(Mishnah, Gittin, 14 10)*

This was a time when many frivolous divorces for unworthy reasons were a great injustice against women.[2] Women were being brutally kicked out of the marital home and left to the mercy of a world without the welfare state we enjoy today, perhaps becoming 'damaged goods' that cruel men could do with as they please. This woman knew full well that a lover, or even a husband, didn't equate to a true and fully satisfying love. She was isolated, judged and down-trodden. Even if we take the interpretation kindest to her past husbands, they had died and left her alone and financially wrecked. It was extremely unusual for a woman to have six marital-type relationships; three seems to be the maximum recorded at this time.[3] I imagine she and others thought there was something wrong with her; why else would these repeated tragedies keep happening?

Psychologist and theologian Edward T. Welch describes shame as a profound feeling of being unacceptable due to actions you have taken, things that have been done to you, or your associations. This leads to feelings of exposure and humiliation. To put it more strongly, you experience disgrace because you behaved inhumanely, were treated inhumanely, or were linked to something inhumane, all under the watchful eyes of others.[4] I believe the woman at the well ticked all three boxes; to what degree, only God knows. Her shame was probably a combination of her own sin (we have all fallen short of the glory of God, Rom. 3:23) and, undoubtedly, being sinned against and having vulnerability taken advantage of. If she were alive today, she'd have a fair few #metoo and #churchtoo tags to her name.

The Samaritan woman's search for love had led to shame and feeling socially trapped. Yet Jesus brought her love and freedom. He had no need for a soul mate, no need for her to complete him in any way, and no one would have pegged them as 'the perfect fit', and yet his love healed her broken heart, lifted her head and gave her confidence to re-engage with her community.

Jesus progressively reveals his identity throughout this encounter, and so that's what we're going to think about next in three sections: our all-seeing, all-knowing, all-mighty God.

All-seeing: Jesus comes with compassion

Sometimes I sneak into our kids' bedrooms when they're asleep at night to look at them just because I love them. I rearrange my work diary to leave early some days so I can see them at their gymnastics or tennis clubs, or I take Holly out in our lunch breaks. They are filled with joy that I have come to see them. That God would make an effort to truly see us and then stay in a relationship with us once our blemishes are revealed is evidence of his love and delight in us and the security we can find in our relationship with him.

Unlike with a spouse or boyfriend, God's seeing of us isn't dependent on our ability or willingness to make ourselves seen. We may wait until the lights go out to let our tears silently fall in bed at night, but God's love isn't limited by our attempts to hide.

John 4:4 states that Jesus 'had' to go through Samaria. I can't prove it, but I sense he had to meet with the woman at the well. The suffering she was experiencing because of her shame compelled him to go. He saw her and loved her with too much devotion to leave her believing that she was alone or unseen. It was a divine appointment.

A brilliant writer on John's Gospel, Ian Galloway, helped me to see the connection between our story, and what happened many, many years earlier by another kind of well, a spring of water in the wilderness. Vulnerable, pregnant servant Hagar was on the run from having been harshly treated by her mistress, Sarah. She was alone, afraid and ashamed, perhaps from being pressured to sleep with her mistress's husband, Abraham. God tenderly met with her and compassionately cared for her. He gave her the privilege of naming him.

'You are a God of seeing' she said, calling him 'Beer-lahai-roi', which means, 'the well of the Living One who sees me' (Gen. 16:13–14).

Jesus' previous, one-to-one interaction in John's Gospel was with Nicodemus. He was a respected, male, Jewish rabbi and a member of the ruling council. By contrast, here is an unnamed woman of suspicious moral standing from a nowhere town. She's a Samaritan, an ethnic enemy of the Jews. The Jews looked down on Samaritans for historically mixing with pagans, with some even seeing them as 'half-breeds'. Yet John 4:42 highlights that Jesus is the Saviour who sees the need within us all – regardless of whether you are a 'good girl' or not. Jesus crossed cultural boundaries to show that no one is excluded from his love. As a male, Jewish rabbi, he would be criticized for sitting with her. Counter-culturally, Jesus introduced himself in the gentlest way possible by asking for her help (even though he arguably didn't really need it; he is the 'I am' God in need of nothing, see v. 26).

When we are consumed by a hidden darkness, regret or fear, Jesus' reaction is not one of shock or social distance. Instead, he draws closer and sits next to us even when all others struggle to embrace us. The deeper we've sunk, the more he will lean in with love to raise us up again.

When the woman hears what Jesus can provide – living water – she recognizes her need and asks him for it in verse 15. To be married is a joy, but it can't fulfil our deepest needs. A husband can serve you, but he can never rescue you from your sin. A husband can encourage you, but he can't cleanse you. He can protect you, but he cannot be a refuge and high tower like God can (Ps. 18:2). He will hopefully love you, but his love will always lack the depth, persistence, and power of

God's love. If you are married and now beginning to doubt whether your husband is enough for you, you're on the right track. This is not a message to abandon marriage but to put it in its proper place. We need to love and cling to our divine husband, Christ, first and above all others. He is the only one who can complete and fulfil us; and without him the gift of marriage becomes a broken cistern – appearing to hold life-giving water, yet unable to truly satisfy.

All-knowing: Jesus accepts with agape love

Acceptance is the answer to rejection. Lots of us wrestle with the fear of rejection and feel imprisoned by it. Rejection and shame hang out together like best friends, actually, it's more as though they're an 'item'. We think that the solution to avoiding rejection is projecting perfection, but Jesus shows us that freedom comes from bringing the darkness we're trying to hide into the light through confession and honesty. Jesus is much more interested in our messy, sinful true selves than the masks we project.

> 'Go, call your husband . . .' he says.
> 'I have no husband,' she replies.
> 'Ahh,' Jesus, I imagine, says knowingly, smiling. 'You are right in saying, "I have no husband"; for you have had five husbands, and the one you now have is not your husband. What you have said is true.'
>
> *(John 4:16–18, paraphrased)*

Jesus is exposing her painful past, but not in a cruel way. He's gently helping her to own it, which she implicitly does by responding, 'I perceive that you are a prophet' (v. 19). I think she's saying, 'You are right about me.'

Jesus is leading her into everlasting life. He continues to talk with her about true worship and privileges her above so many others by revealing his true identity as the Messiah – the one who comes to put all things right. He also calls himself the 'I AM' – referencing the name of God revealed to Moses (Exod. 3:14). You might even say he is wooing her. And in a way, you wouldn't be wrong.

Throughout Scripture, wells are meeting places that lead to marriage. For example, a wife was found for Isaac at a well (Gen. 24), and Moses first met the brothers of his wife-to-be at a well (Exod. 2:15–21). John specifically reminds us of this connection by pointing out that this true event in the life of Jesus is unfolding at Jacob's well, hyperlinking us back to Genesis 29, where Jacob first met his wife, Rachel. The Samaritan woman could be seen to figuratively represent Jewish and Gentile unfaithfulness, going as far back as the disobedient ten northern tribes of Israel, and their subsequent intermixing with pagan non-Jews, originally Assyrians (see 2 Kgs 17:24–41). Now, if we add the five husbands this woman had to the man she's currently with; that makes six, right? Note also that the number seven in the Jewish-Christian context speaks of completion, even perfection (from the seventh day of creation on which God rested and celebrated his creative work). So Jesus, having just been referred to as the 'bridegroom' in the preceding chapter (John 3:29), is coming as the six-plus-one (himself), seventh husband. He's the perfect, faithful husband who never kicks you out or lets you down. He's like a true and better Hosea reaching out to unfaithful wife Gomer (figuratively, the people of God), alluring her and speaking 'tenderly to her' (Hos. 2:14). His unconditional love turns our valleys of sinful trouble into doorways of happy hope. Isn't this a picture of Jesus wooing the bride of Christ, his Jewish-Gentile church?

It's also a true story about his love for you as an individual. He accepts you. He says, 'I do, and I won't even let death part us if you will just receive me.' But we can make receiving trickier than it needs to be. We think we need to make more of ourselves for him to accept us; but our relationship with the bridegroom is manifestly unfair. We give him our heart and our sin, and he gives us everything. Everlasting life, every good spiritual gift, the maintenance of creation itself; everything comes from God.

In this way, the woman at the well had a head start when she met Jesus because she knew how little she had to offer God as well as her supreme need for him. Those of us who enjoy a reasonably good ranking in society can find recognizing the extent of our need trickier. We who have been trained that good things come to those who work hard can be tempted to earn his love or feel the need to build up an offering of good works to counter our sin before we admit it. Or even sometimes to reflect on our achievements and think, 'Jesus chose a good one in me.' Instead, Jesus loves to embrace and love those who see how empty their hands are. He is willing to bring it all to the table.

All-mighty: Jesus builds up for breakthrough

Jesus empowers for harvest (see the references to harvest and mission in John 4:35–8). What happens next in the story is profoundly moving. The Samaritan woman runs to the very people she has been hiding from to tell them about Jesus. What a transformation! I imagine her jumping with joy, unable to get the words out fast enough – she is just so excited. She testifies: 'He told me all that I ever did' (v. 39b). This is strange because he didn't. Jesus had sensitively told her only about her relationships. But it's as if this so defined her it had become her identity, and her faith in Jesus had made her new. Her history was no longer a cause for shame but celebration. Her past didn't define her any more, and her transformation touched an entire town as many came to believe that Jesus is the Saviour of the World.

Most happy couples will at some point reach a time where they desire to have children. Holly and I reached that point just over ten years ago. I'm not sure either of us could ever explain to you exactly why we wanted them, but there is something that compels you to want to bring others into the joy of your mini family and to raise little people to know the love you have received. The same is meant to be true for the bride, the church, and her bridegroom, Jesus. So wonderful is his love, it should compel us to want others to know that same love and salvation, to be brought into the family of God's church.

Please notice as well that it's through the Samaritan woman's very weakness that God displayed his strength. Her story of vulnerability and struggle is where he revealed his power. And likewise, God's glory, his great goodness, will be more visible through our weakness. We don't have to be experts at evangelism; we don't have to have savings accounts, good jobs or houses to bring to the table of this relationship.

When Jesus asks the woman at the well for a drink, she replies in verse 9, 'How?' She is asking, 'How can I enter into even a distant, transactional, relational encounter with you? Do you not realize who I am?'

But we see that God wants to turn our *how* questions into *who* answers. He responds in verse 10, 'If you knew the gift of God, and who it is that is saying to you, "Give me a drink", you would have asked him, and he would have given you living water.' It's as though he's saying, 'If you realize who I really am – God – you'd know you don't need to worry about the how; nothing is impossible for me.'

We just have to recognize who he is and ask him, to be saved. We just have to sit with him and allow him to transform us with his healing love, to be empowered to tell others about him. Many from Sychar, nearly that entire town, came to faith because of this unnamed woman's willingness to testify. She encouraged them to see for themselves, to taste and see that the Lord is good. She became an early example of the role of an evangelist; someone special Jesus wanted his disciples to emulate.

Jesus was no stranger to social rejection himself, most notably from the religious leaders who should have been the first to recognize and worship him. In this, I am in awe of the emotional strength of our Saviour, who walked the path of suffering without absorbing the label of shame. To mention just three examples: his hometown disbelieved him and tried to throw him down a cliff (Luke 4:16–30); Peter denied knowing him during his hardest moments (Luke 22:54–62); and during his crucifixion, he was mocked (Luke 23:36–8). Many of us struggle to process an odd look we're given without spiralling into self-rejection and shame. But Jesus not only moved towards people who had been rejected like the woman at the well, he also refused to allow the world to isolate or control his own actions by their scorn or rejection of himself.

In Hebrews 12:2, we gain great insight into Jesus' motivation and emotional strength: 'who for the joy that was set before him endured the cross, despising the shame'. What was the joy that enabled him to endure such unjust suffering? What was the joy that enabled him to think so little of the extreme shame of being spat upon and dying as a reprehensible criminal? Or, in other words, when Jesus cried out from the cross, 'I thirst' (John 19:28), echoing John 4:7, 'Give me a drink' – what is he really thirsting for?

The answer is his bride, believers, shameful women and men like you and me. It is his joy to transform our lives, to take the shame of our sin upon himself so we can go free. That is what the cross was about. Don't scorn Jesus, like so many do today. Scorn your shame instead. Think little of it by thinking much of him. He is the all-seeing, all-knowing, all-powerful God. And he loves you with the truest love you could ever know.

The woman at the well left her water jar behind in John 4:28. It's an important detail. She didn't need it any more. She had Jesus' better, living water, his love to sustain her. He was more than enough for her now. He completed her. He will complete you, too and, in doing so, help you to leave behind what doesn't.

Questions for reflection

With what relationship shame do you wrestle? How does it isolate you?

How does Jesus truly seeing, understanding and lovingly accepting you (including your most sensitive shameful parts) touch your heart?

What broken cisterns do you need to stop drinking from? What do you need to leave behind to obey Jesus today?

How will you invite people to come and see Jesus this week? What could your testimony be?

LYDIA

Boss Lady

Bible study

Read

Acts 16:11-15

Context

Jesus has died and been resurrected and ascended to God in heaven. Paul and Silas have been working together as missionaries, revisiting the churches from Paul's first mission, and Timothy has joined them. Then, Paul received a call from God to go to Macedonia through a vision. Luke has likely joined them by the time they meet Lydia, as the narrative starts using the pronoun 'we'.

Study and write

- What can we tell about Lydia from this passage?

- What impact did Paul's gospel message have on her? What was her reaction?

- How is God's goodness shown through this passage?

Pray and reflect

- Think about your work (in the workplace or the home) and ask God to give you a godly vision for how it contributes to his kingdom purposes.

- Thank God that when you seek him, he answers you and that he has a plan and purpose for you.

Thoughts on Lydia

Sometimes life goes our way. Sometimes in a big way, or at least just enough to earn you a #thisgirlcan badge and a little awed respect among your friendship circle. As I write this chapter, it's International Women's Day, and the London *Metro* newspaper on the train seat next to me is full of articles listing women at the top of their game or expertise. I'll admit that as I reflected on my previous attempt at self-employment, I felt a little inept in contrast as I read about their determination and business acumen. Yet somewhere in the depths of my anxiety, a small, often-crushed voice of self-belief speaks a bit louder as a result of their inspiration.

The world, and history, are full of impressive women: creative, intelligent, business-minded women. Next week our children's school is celebrating science week, and my daughter is dressing up as Marie Curie. Marie, a Polish scientist, discovered polonium and radium. She directed the first studies into using radioactive isotopes to treat neoplasms and developed mobile radiography units so that X-rays could be taken in field hospitals during World War 1. She received two Nobel Prizes in different fields of science. Marie Curie was a boss lady.

I had a private coaching client, a Christian, who had excelled in law and was facing the responsibility and financial rewards of partnership. A friend won a national singing competition and played leading roles in top musicals in London and New York. All around us, we will know women who have thrived in the workplace – boss ladies, or at least ladies with nice handbags who holiday abroad. Maybe you are one of these women, still climbing a ladder but enjoying the view you've managed to achieve to date.

Lydia was one of these. She knew success as defined by the world. She was a boss lady. In a time when it was hard to make it as a woman in many career paths other than midwifery, Lydia had an enviable business selling purple cloth. She was from Thyatira, a place well-known for its notable guilds, including that of dyers, because its water was so well-adapted for some of the most luxurious dyes.[1] Tyrian purple was a dye made from marine molluscs, and it was particularly expensive. Only the wealthiest clients would have been able to afford her products and, given that she seemed to own her own spacious home and was attended to by multiple servants, we can assume that her business was prospering. Lydia was an astute businesswoman, living and working in a material world (excuse the pun), pro-actively tap-tapping away at glass ceilings. But, as we'll see, Lydia's heart wasn't ultimately in the world; it was in her Lord.

As some navigate the privilege of worldly success, the end goal can become clouded. As we fight our way through gender pay gaps and biases, which can label the assertive as difficult and the nurturing as too emotional or soft, our eyes can easily be pulled inward and downward. We can forget whether the destination is crushing the glass ceiling or if that is a by-product of the journey to getting somewhere or something else. Is equal pay the solution, or is it a way of working out a deeper truth that we long for the world to hear? Do we not deserve the same pay and respect because we are both made in the image of God by the Creator who values us so much that he would sacrifice his own Son to rescue us both?

Being divine glory-bringers in the workplace is not usually as exciting or heroic as it reads. As the meetings, projects, reports and emails pile up, we can begin to doubt what kingdom-effect the time we plough into our careers really has and how 'ministry' could ever apply to this contract negotiation or coming school inspection. Additionally, as the material comforts or opportunities open to us, we can stealthily slip into the temptation of thinking we deserve them and that we can do just fine on our own. Unconsciously, we can begin to put our hope in 'success' as our salvation over and above our Saviour.

Interestingly, the story of Lydia is followed in the book of Acts by the narrative of a slave girl (Acts 16:16–24). This girl wasn't anywhere near glass ceilings; she was at the bottom of the corporate food chain. She also made good money, but the two men who owned her took advantage of the demonic spirit of divination that possessed her. She didn't see the financial rewards she was agonizingly amassing for them, and the two men couldn't see – or chose not to value – the girl's agony behind the finances they enjoyed. Material success had become their goal, and fortune was their moral compass. This girl was 'their hope of gain' and the gospel an unwelcome disturbance to the city (Acts 16:19). Their indulgent gains had become their security and purpose – in an instant, God showed them how foolish that focus, that false saviour, had been. Fortune is power, control and certainty to the world, but to God it's a grace-filled gift, which the flick of his hand can redirect to make space for the greater gospel gift to be known.

Do we live only in a material world?

The enslavers thought they were living in a material world, a world where money pulled all the strings in life, but Lydia had realized that life was deeper and more complex than that. Her home, servants and business were not all she needed. They weren't her strength for the day, her hope for the future, or her life's overarching purpose. She almost certainly saw through the potential power plays that may have been open to her to the sovereignty of our Creator God who holds the universe together. Throughout history, this has always been a physical and spiritual world. God controls the cosmos; the earth will melt at an utterance of his voice (Ps. 46:6), and he shapes the insignificant day to day; not even a sparrow, bought with one of the least valuable Roman coins, will fall to the ground outside of his control (Matt. 10:29–31). Job rebukes his friend Bildad with these words:

> The dead tremble
>> under the waters and their inhabitants.
> Sheol is naked before God,
>> and Abaddon has no covering.
> He stretches out the north over the void
>> and hangs the earth on nothing.
> He binds up the waters in his thick clouds,
>> and the cloud is not split open under them.
> He covers the face of the full moon
>> and spreads over it his cloud.
> He has inscribed a circle on the face of the waters
>> at the boundary between light and darkness.
> The pillars of heaven tremble
>> and are astounded at his rebuke.
> By his power he stilled the sea;
>> by his understanding he shattered Rahab.[2]
> By his wind the heavens were made fair;
>> his hand pierced the fleeing serpent.

Behold, these are but the outskirts of his ways,
    and how small a whisper do we hear of him!
But the thunder of his power who can understand?

Job 26:5–14

There is much that we do not understand this side of eternity. Don't let the noise of worldly success drown out the whisper that we can hear, such that you might miss the reality of his God's thunderous power and love. Do you think he is even the tiniest bit intimidated or restricted by your impressive promotions, academic achievements, or your CEO's position on the Fortune 500 list? Many of us may bat away that question because for most of us our idolatry is more subtle than that. What if I asked you whether you tithe/give, or how much? How reasonable are your anxiety levels when you have a tight month? Or how do you feel when you think about the cost of your children attending university? How much more do you admire and aspire to be like your friends with social or career influence over other friends who are ploughing away to provide the basics for their families? God's glory is not limited or curtailed by the material or financial world we live in. He offers us security that runs deeper than our bank balance.

Before Lydia accepted the gospel, she is described as 'a worshipper of God' (Acts 16:14). There seems to be some debate as to whether Lydia was Jewish or had adopted the Jewish faith as a Gentile,[3] but what is clear is that she sought God. She couldn't find the answer to her questions or hopes in this material world or her proven ability. 'Success' in itself didn't satisfy. Instead, despite the lack of a synagogue, she gathered with the other women who worshipped God at a place of prayer by the riverside on the Sabbath.[4] When Paul and

Silas talk with her, and the Lord opens her heart, she and her household are quickly baptized.

Lydia was a trader; she was used to assessing value and assigning price tags. In Jesus, Lydia knew that she had found something, someone, worth more than anything the world could offer her, and there was no worthy price tag to assign to the grace he had given her. Jesus didn't demand a price tag; the gift of salvation to Lydia was free and hers regardless of what she did with her resources. But the gospel was Lydia's treasure, and she chose to do all she could to make sure others shared in this precious gift too.

Is God's glory incompatible with worldly success?

When Lydia gave her life to Jesus, she gave all of it without holding back. But for Lydia, giving away didn't mean giving up. Jesus called the fishermen to drop their nets and follow him, but he had a different call for Lydia. Her work continued, but now it was reframed with a different endgame, a different form of success; Lydia worked for the gospel now.

Lydia opens her home and shows wonderful hospitality and generosity, even after Paul and Silas are discharged from prison. Her role in the church itself isn't certain, but her support and patronage clearly enables the gospel to continue to spread throughout Philippi, and her fellowship is deeply valued by Paul and Silas.

A.W. Tozer encourages us with the helpful principle that it is not what we do that determines whether our work is secular or sacred, but why we do it.[5] Lydia's work continues but her business has a new vision and purpose. She is still a successful lady, but she now operates her business under a boss, the

Triune God, whose plans are higher and better than hers. I love that when we become believers, we don't join the Borg Collective and are coercively conformed and assimilated into a hive mind (my husband loves that I got his *Star Trek* reference in here!). Instead, God has creatively made us to be unique with our own skill sets and personalities, which he wants us to keep using and developing.

Unlike the rich young man in Matthew 19:16–30 and Mark 10:17–31, who mourned the prospect of losing his possessions, Lydia possessed resources – but she didn't put her love or hope in them. Her success in business wasn't a way of fuelling a love or dependency on the reputational or monetary rewards that her business brought her. As 1 Timothy 6:10 warns us, the love of money is the root of all kinds of evil and a wandering faith. I believe this is a principle that helps illuminate God's view of our particular success. We need to be ready to ask ourselves where our treasure truly resides.

I make a lot of decisions based on our bank balance; whether to put our children into swimming lessons, whether we can book a holiday, and how many times we eat meat a week. The list goes on endlessly. Our finances are actual. If I went on a shopping spree and maxed out my cards, the consequences of that would be very real. Equally, I make a lot of decisions based on my work: whether I have time to take on an additional commitment, what study or advertising to pay for, and how to build a useful professional network of people. Unlike me, God is not constrained in any way by the reality of commerce and price tags or the human structures and constructs of workplaces.

God is the source of all things. He isn't constrained by the hoops my client must jump through to become a partner or the qualifications a family member needs for her professorship at an art college. He wasn't in need of Lydia's wealth to grow fledging believers into the famous church at Philippi. This is the God who made a donkey talk (Num. 22:28), preserved Shadrach, Meshach and Abednego unharmed in a furnace of flames (Dan. 3:8–27), and freed an entire nation of slaves (worth a fortune to ancient Egypt) through plagues (Exod. 7 – 10). Instead, we see God *choose* to work through Lydia and her generosity, and within the financial reality we experience to accomplish his purposes.

Why? Because in bypassing these with his divinity, he would take away our opportunity to learn, grow and know him more intimately. This narrative shows us that God isn't interested in amassing grey, faceless numbers; he wants a relationship with us. He wants to help us develop into the flourishing people he created us to be, and he wants us to learn the joy of living a life dependent on him. He wants to be a part of our job applications, medical exams and profit analysis because it is part of how he disciples us.

The young rich man was asked to sell his possessions, and the fishermen were told to give up their nets, because that was needed for them to be discipled. It was needed for them to learn to put their love, security and hope in God alone. For Lydia, whose heart was already worshipping God, keeping her business was as much a discipleship opportunity. It was a chance to learn how to pursue business along gospel, grace-filled principles and to see that the profits had always ultimately belonged to the Lord. Her success was an opportunity to learn that lives being transformed and saved by the gospel is more joyful than any prominent heir or heiress wearing her cloth.

God offers us eternity with him, and that starts now, not once we die. He's interested in our development and work now too. He doesn't have a desperate need for hands on the ground but, in a rich display of compassion, God, in all his glory and might, slows and stoops to work within our red tape and interest rates to help teach us to safeguard our faith and keep our feet upon the true Rock, our greatest gain.

The mercy of God

This coming Sunday, it's Mother's Day, and I'm preaching at our church. Every time I speak, I struggle with anxiety. I have even been known to have mini panic attacks in the days leading up to the service. I practise deep breathing like an Olympic swimmer and have worship music on a constant loop, half hoping Amazon's Alexa can emit into me some special anointing. I want people to know Jesus, and I don't want to come up short on stage.

Paul was obedient to share the gospel with the women at the riverside, but Lydia's conversion didn't come from fancy words.[6] Acts 16:14 makes it clear that 'The Lord opened her heart to pay attention'. The Lord – not impressive lexical knowledge or powerful metaphors – in his mercy and desire to save, opens her heart to consider this gospel message. He doesn't leave the heavy lifting to Paul and this team alone. He cares too much for his lost sheep. We anxiously and arrogantly think that we can single-handedly persuade another heart into surrender, or we become self-righteous that we saw Jesus when others couldn't. Yet salvation doesn't come through our work but by God's intervention to change hearts. In our own salvation and in our sharing of the gospel to others, only God can change a human soul.[7]

God is merciful to save. God is also merciful and good in how he saves because we are rarely easy projects but demand his patience and perseverance. My story is not Lydia's story. It took several conversations over many years for me to accept the truth that God had opened my heart to and, thereafter, I had a couple of wobbles. Lydia accepted Jesus quickly, but the effort needed to get Paul and Silas to her wasn't insignificant.

At a time when travel was often difficult and lengthy, the missionary journeys in Acts are incredible, particularly Paul's. After Paul was given a vision telling him to go to Macedonia (Acts 16:9–10), he and Silas crossed the sea and journeyed many hours from Samothrace to Neapolis, to Philippi. This would have been quite an upheaval. Yet when they arrive, there is no one to receive them in the city; no synagogue, let alone a church. They have to leave the city and go to the riverside to find anyone ready to hear their message. This is a sweet, intimate insight into Lydia's relationship with God that she would go to such an effort to seek him, and him to meet with her.

Calvin argues these brief verses speak of God's pattern of seeking out the small, working with a seemingly humble and weak appearance, so that we can more easily see his glory and power.[8] Lydia was one woman who quickly grew to one household, that became one of the most well-known early churches.

Lastly, I think we often miss the mercy of God while spending so much time with people who are successful in the worldly sense. In a culture driven by achievement and independence, we are rightly moved by the fact that God would delight in and love someone like the unnamed bleeding woman, or the slave girl freed from a divination spirit. We stand in awe that the perfect Creator of the universe would have time for the lowest, most broken and least accomplished of us because this is so different from how we might direct our relational efforts. But from heaven's perspective, I often wonder if the miracle can often be the reverse.

When my finances are tight or a family member is ill, I pray and cry out to God with an intense passion. We often make time for God when our need for him confronts us inescapably in the face, but when it's more hidden, his relevance can sometimes feel more distant. When we appear to be thriving materially and are surrounded by people who care for us, prioritizing time with our Heavenly Father can easily slip. God, however, always has time for us. He always seeks us. That God would reach out to us when we see no need for him is miraculous to me. While we are so vulnerable to distraction, he never loses sight of the rescue that we need – whether we are in plenty or want. His view of reality isn't reframed by how we currently feel about our life but instead is informed by a perfect, eternal perspective that can see only goodness once we are washed in the blood of the lamb, Jesus (Rev. 7:14).

Lydia was a successful woman who was seeking God. She had noticed her need. Have you?

Questions for reflection

How have you known success (family, work, friend-ships, finance, church, etc.)?

In what do you default to putting your security and hope? To put it another way, where is your treasure today?

Do you connect the gospel with your work and fi-nancial provision? If so, how?

How does knowing that God isn't limited by our fi-nancial reality strengthen your faith?

Final Words

The story of God's glory and our womanhood could span hundreds of books. We have just skimmed the surface of his goodness here with a tiny sprinkle of some of the multitude of themes and seasons our life experience can bring us. We have picked out a small handful of the many women God included in Scripture.

Being a woman is a beautiful gift. It is good because God chooses it to be. It feels tempting to end this book with a triumphant declaration of the glory of womanhood, but doing so would undermine the core thread I hope has been the heartbeat through every chapter: God alone is good and glorious. Our lives are much less about us than we give them credit, they orbit around a much greater story that spans history and geography. This greater gospel, while often ignored in our culture, still saturates the world and pulsates through our own experiences.

Even when we choose to run away and resist God, his glory persists. In truth, without God's grace, we are all living out Gomer's narrative. She was a prostitute whom God asked Hosea, in the book of the same name, to marry and love. Despite his ardent attempts to love her, she kept running away and being with other men. Hosea, as a picture of God running after his church, constantly took her back and persistently loved her despite all her hurtful rebellion against him.

Like Hosea, God's beautiful relentless love selflessly chases after us. It chases us as we stubbornly think that we can walk this life better on our own terms. It chases us when we shun God's good glory, and it chases us when we accept him but struggle not to pursue him alongside so many other loves. We cannot outrun God's love; it pursues us with unlimited strength and endurance.

Our womanhood is also not just a gift, it is a spiritual weapon. In every season, joy or challenge, it declares God's character and glory in a multitude of different ways for those who will open their eyes to see it; as you cradle your nursing baby or make wise business decisions that honour his kingdom. Even as you pop some paracetamol for period pain, there is a message in your womanhood – as there is in manhood too – about who God is that the world needs to hear. Without both these sides of the coin coming together, we will always lack some depth in our understanding of who God is and just how much he loves us.

To finish, a word of advice, something which I have tried to avoid throughout the rest of the book. When we are young, we assume we will 'figure it out' and clear the messy mist of our questions as we age, but mostly life just gets more complicated. Learning to be a woman is an ever-evolving, lifelong journey, partly because our womanhood isn't static. Expectations and health come and go. Things we aspired to become less possible, and others become more so. Our entire physicality goes through monumental changes (which often in turn affect us mentally as well) multiple times. So, as old questions are answered, new ones emerge.

However, God's unbounded glory seemingly grows with our own lives and questions. We can't control life and it doesn't always give us what we want, but God is always good; not tame or mouldable, not driven by the same desires as us, but good. So remind yourself often to look for him, even in the most unlikely of places, such as fear and the menopause, because his goodness resides just as steadily in even the most remote crevices. He is with us now and always, and his glory awaits us face to face one day.

> Surely goodness and mercy shall follow me
> all the days of my life
> and I shall dwell in the house of the Lord for ever.
>
> *(Ps. 23:6)*

Take off the mask and breathe, my friend, because the Glorious One loves you: steadfast and for ever.

Notes

Introduction

1. Dane Ortlund, *Gentle and Lowly* (Wheaton: Crossway, 2020), p. 147.
2. D.F. Kelly, P.B. Rollinson and F.T. Marsh, eds, *The Westminster Shorter Catechism in Modern English* (Phillipsburg, NJ: Presbyterian & Reformed Pub. Co., 1986), Question 1.

1   Afraid of the Dark – Hagar

1. Office for National Statistics, 'Perceptions of Personal Safety and Experiences of Harassment', data from the Opinions and Lifestyle Survey in Great Britain: 16 February to 13 March 2022 https://www.ons.gov.uk/peoplepopulationandcommunity/crimeandjustice/bulletins/perceptionsofpersonalsafetyandexperiencesofharassmentgreatbritain/16februaryto13march2022 (accessed 6 Jan. 2025).
2. John Calvin, *Genesis* (Edinburgh and Pennsylvania: Banner of Truth Trust, 1975; reprinted from Calvin translation edn of 1847), p. 423.
3. For ease, I will refer to them as Sarah and Abraham from now onwards, despite their names still being Sarai and Abram throughout Genesis 16.
4. In Gen. 21:17 he asks her what 'troubles' her and reassures her to 'fear not'.
5. Calvin, *Genesis*, p. 433.
6. Saugato Biswas, 'A Curious Case of Sweating Blood', *Indian Journal of Dermatology* (Nov.–Dec. 2023) https://www.ncbi.nlm.nih.gov/pmc/articles/PMC3827523 (accessed 6 Jan. 2025).
7. Phil. 4:19; Matt. 6:24–34; Rom. 8:31–2; Eph. 3:20; Ps. 34:9–10; Luke 11:5–11.
8. Interestingly, Abraham is buried in Genesis 25 by both Isaac and Ishmael, suggesting that Isaac and Ishmael were reunited at some point before Abraham's death.

2 I am Mother, Hear Me Roar – Jochebed

1 Isa. 64:8; Mal. 2:10; Matt. 23:9; John 14:9–11 and 1 Cor. 8:6 are examples among many.
2 *Seven Pounds* (Sony Pictures Entertainment, 2008).
3 Tim Mackie, Jonathan Collins and Carissa Quinn, 'The Womb of God?' *BibleProject Podcast* (31 Aug. 2020) https://bibleproject.com/podcast/the-womb-of-god (accessed 6 Jan. 2025).
4 Glen Scrivener, *The Air We Breathe* (Surrey: Good Book, 2022), p. 184.
5 Gal. 4:26–7 helps us understand that it is the church that is being described in Isa. 66:7–14.

3 The Decisions that Make Us – Rahab

1 Dr Joel Hoomans, '35,000 Decisions: The Great Choices of Strategic Leaders', *The Leading Edge*, Roberts Wesleyan University (Mar. 2015) https://go.roberts.edu/leadingedge/the-great-choices-of-strategic-leaders (accessed 6 Jan. 2025).
2 John C. Maxwell, *Beyond Talent: Become Someone Who Gets Extraordinary Results* (Nashville, TN: Thomas Nelson, 2011), p. 10.
3 Hannah Anderson, *All That's Good* (Chicago: Moody, 2018), p. 57.
4 John Piper, 'A Beginner's Guide to "Free Will"', *Desiring God* (July 2016) https://www.desiringgod.org/articles/a-beginners-guide-to-free-will (accessed 6 Jan. 2025).
5 Thomas Brooks, *The Select Works of The Rev. Thomas Brooks* (London: L.B. Seeley & Son, 1824), p. 477.
6 1 Clem. 12:7, found in F.F. Bruce, *The Epistle to the Hebrews* (Grand Rapids, MI: Eerdmans, 1974), p. 329. This refers to the First Epistle of Clement, which was most likely written by Clement (the fourth bishop of Rome) to the Christians in Corinth during the late first century. It is not part of canonical Scripture but is one of the earliest preserved Christian letters outside of the New Testament.
7 Phil Moore, *Joshua, Judges and Ruth* (Oxford: Monarch), 2018), p. 23.
8 Minnie E. Paull (also Mrs George A. Paull) printed in *Ye Nexte Thynge* by Eleanor Amerman Sutphen (New York, Toronto, Chicago: Fleming H. Revell, 1897).

4 The Importance of the Ordinary – Ruth

[1] Eugene H. Peterson, *A Long Obedience in the Same Direction: Discipleship in an Instant Society* (Downers Grove, IL: InterVarsity Press, 1980), p. 16.
[2] Tish Harrison Warren, *Liturgy of the Ordinary* (Downers Grove, IL: InterVarsity Press, 2016), p. 84.
[3] Leland Ryken, James C. Wilhoit and Tremper Longman III, *Dictionary of Biblical Imagery* (Downers Grove, IL: InterVarsity Press, 1998), p. 745.
[4] James Bejon, 'Ruth, Boaz and the Redemption of the Past', *Academia* (Dec. 2020) https://www.academia.edu/39775654/Ruth_Boaz_and_the_Redemption_of_the_Past (accessed 6 Jan. 2025).

5 Growing Up: Not Just a Girl Any More – Esther

[1] Charles R. Swindoll, *Esther: A Woman of Strength and Dignity: Profiles in Character* (Nashville, TN: W Publishing Group, 1997), p. 7.
[2] David G. Firth, *The Message of Esther* (Nottingham: Inter-Varsity Press, 2010), pp. 48–9 and 56–8; Swindoll, *Esther*, pp. 1–2.
[3] Laurence A. Turner, 'Desperately Seeking YHWH: Finding God in Esther's "Acrostics"', *Academia* (2013) https://www.academia.edu/6370833/Desperately_Seeking_YHWH_Finding_God_in_Esthers_Acrostics (accessed 6 Jan. 2025).
[4] Firth, *Message of Esther*, pp. 59–69.
[5] Firth, *Message of Esther*, p. 53.
[6] C.S. Lewis, *The Weight of Glory* (California: HarperOne, 2001), p. 26.
[7] Herbert Lockyer, *All the Women of the Bible* (Grand Rapids, MI: Zondervan, 1967), p. 54.
[8] A.W. Tozer, *The Pursuit of God: The Human Thirst for the Divine* (Camp Hills, PA: WingSpread, 1982), p. 70.
[9] Clare Heath-Whyte, *Everyone a Child Should Know* (Lancashire: 10Publishing, 2017), p. 15.

6 Unexpected Endings – Anna

[1] Lockyer, *All the Women*, p. 29; Bible Hub (2004–24) https://biblehub.com/greek/5323.htm (accessed 6 Jan. 2025).

2   Phrase borrowed from book title: Kate Bowler, *No Cure for Being Human (and Other Truths I Need to Hear)* (London: Penguin, 2021).

3   Bowler, *No Cure*, p. 186.

4   William Jay, *Lectures on Female Scripture Characters* (independently published, rev. edn, 2019), p. 98. (Originally published London: Hamilton, Adams & Co., 1754.)

5   This idea comes from a seminar given by Andrew and Rachel Wilson at Westpoint, a Commission family weekend away in 2018, when unpacking their book, *The Life You Never Expected: Thriving While Parenting Special Needs Children* (London: Inter-Varsity Press, 2015).

6   John Flavel, *Keeping the Heart: How to Maintain Your Love for God* (Fearn, Scotland: Christian Focus, rev. edn. 2012), p. 43.

7   Mary Ann Getty-Sullivan, *Women in the New Testament* (Collegeville, MN: Liturgical Press, 2001), p. 37.

7   Blood, Sweat and Tears – The Bleeding Woman

1   Rachel Jones, *A Brief Theology of Periods (Yes, Really)* (Surrey, UK: Good Book, 2021), p. 89.

2   '7 Amazing Facts about Periods Everyone Needs to Know', *Helping Women Period* (2019) https://www.helpingwomenperiod.org/7-amazing-facts-about-periods-that-everyone-needs-to-know (accessed 6 Jan. 2025).

3   United Nations Population Division, 'Fertility rate, total (births per woman)' *World Bank Group* (2022) https://data.worldbank.org/indicator/sp.dyn.tfrt.in (accessed 6 Jan. 2025).

4   Jones, *Brief Theology*, pp. 23–4.

5   Tim Mackie, Jonathan Collins and Carissa Quinn, 'The Womb of God?' *BibleProject Podcast* (31 Aug. 2020) https://bibleproject.com/podcast/the-womb-of-god (accessed 6 Jan. 2025).

6   Jones, *Brief Theology*, p. 43; 1 Tim. 2:15; Gen. 3:15.

7   Just to be clear, as mentioned before, the bleeding didn't make this woman sinful in itself but is a symbol.

8   Dane Ortlund, *Gentle and Lowly* (Wheaton, IL: Crossway, 2020), p. 31.

9   Science Museum, 'Menstruation and Modern Materials', *Science Museum, Objects and Stories* (2020) https://www.sciencemuseum.org.uk/objects-and-stories/everyday-wonders/menstruation-and-modern-materials (accessed 6 Jan. 2025).

[10] William Hendrickson, *New Testament Commentary: Exposition of the Gospel According to Mark* (Grand Rapids, MI: Baker, 2007), p. 206.

[11] Jones, *Brief Theology*, p. 49.

[12] Hendrickson, *New Testament Commentary*, p. 210.

8 Expectations – Mary and Martha

[1] Lockyer, *All the Women*, p. 88.

[2] Phil Moore, *Straight to the Heart of Luke* (Oxford: Monarch, 2017), p. 129.

[3] Ian Galloway, *Called to be Friends* (London: Hodder & Stoughton, 2021), pp. 53–60.

[4] Galloway, *Called to be Friends*, p. 60.

[5] Galloway, *Called to be Friends*, p. 49.

9 Finding True Love – The Woman at the Well

[1] Curt Thomson, *The Soul of Shame: Retelling the Stories We Believe about Ourselves* (Downers Grove, IL: InterVarsity Press, 2015), p. 28 on scrib.

[2] Martyn Lloyd-Jones, *Studies in the Sermon on the Mount* (Nottingham: Inter-Varsity Press, rev. edn, 1976), p. 558.

[3] C. Reeder, *The Samaritan Woman: Reconsidering John 4 after #ChurchToo* (London: Inter-Varsity Press, 2022), p. 149.

[4] Edward T. Welch, *Shame Interrupted: How God Lifts the Pain of Worthlessness and Rejection* (Greensboro, NC: New Growth Press, 2012), p. 2.

10 Boss Lady – Lydia

[1] Lockyer, *All the Women*, p. 84.

[2] God uses Rahab as another name for Egypt. This is not a reference to Rahab in Josh. 2.

[3] For example, John Stott argues that Lydia believed and behaved like a Jew without having become one, hence why she is called a 'worshipper of God' rather than a Jew (John Stott, *The Message of Acts* [Nottingham: Inter-Varsity Press, 1990], p. 263). On the other hand, Calvin asserts

that she must have been a Jewess as it was a capital offence for Greeks and Romans to celebrate the Sabbath, or practise Jewish rites (John Calvin, *Calvin's Commentaries: The Acts of the Apostles 14–28* [trans. John W. Fraser; Edinburgh: Saint Andrew Press, 1966], p. 72).

4   A quorum of ten men was needed to establish a synagogue so we can assume, by the fact that Paul and Silas find all women by the riverside, that a synagogue did not exist in the city and there were not many Jewish males.

5   A.W. Tozer, *The Pursuit of God: The Human Thirst for the Divine* (London: Tate, 2013), p. 90.

6   Stott, *Message of Acts*, p. 263; 1 Cor. 2:1–4.

7   R.C. Sproul, *Acts* (Wheaton, IL: Crossway, 2010), p. 293.

8   Calvin, *Calvin's Commentaries*, p. 71.

Authentic

We trust you enjoyed reading this book
from Authentic. If you want to be
informed of any new titles from this author
and other releases you can sign up to the
Authentic newsletter by scanning below:

Online:
authenticmedia.co.uk

Follow us: